A
WAR
ON
ALL
FRONTS

A WAR ON ALL FRONTS

Anthony P. Johnson, M.A.

E-BookTime, LLC
Montgomery Alabama

A War On All Fronts

Library of Congress Control Number: 2005927169

ISBN: 1-59824-024-2

First Edition
Published May 2005
E-BookTime, LLC
6598 Pumpkin Road
Montgomery, AL 36108
www.e-booktime.com

To Gabriel…the most important person in my life!

Contents

Introduction

As an African American I have endured racism from a wide variety of ethnic groups in the United States. In the last forty years however, the Jewish community has probably been the harshest group at meting out racism towards African Americans. I have had to consistently defend my race because of the negative stereotypes that have been ingrained in the minds of the citizens in this empire we call America. There was a time that the Jewish and African American communities shared a common bond because both experienced such harsh racism not just in America but also throughout the world. Unfortunately, why is it that other ethnic groups who know little or nothing at all about African Americans despise us so? Why are African Americans portrayed negatively on TV. and also in the music industry? Sadly, it is not just here in America, but also on the international stage. In this book I will address the Jewish community and some other ethnic groups in America who African Americans have had to struggle with to break the vicious cycle of stereotypes that have been perceived by their descendants for generations. It is important to note that not all individuals from the various ethnic groups mentioned above in America are racist toward African Americans. My goal by writing this book is to find the origin of racism toward African Americans from these respected ethnic groups. In other words, why did it start? Once the reader reaches the conclusion of this book they will in essence search for solutions in combating racism that permeates this country and abroad. Alas, they will not find it. *A War On All Fronts* tackles the *issue* of racism and not the *solution* to ending it. "Before a cure can be discovered, the disease must first be acknowledged."

I. *Understanding Discrimination Against African Americans*

The term "African American" refers to 33 million people who make up 13% of the U.S. population. Although most are descendants of families that have been in this country for generations, others are recent immigrants from the West Indies, South America, Africa, and the Caribbean. Blacks who immigrate to America do better than blacks that were born and raised in the U.S. Many American blacks have Native American, white, or Latino ancestors. 87% of African Americans live in urban areas, and they are a young population, with a median age of 27, compared to the white median age of 34. Oppressed for over 300 years, discrimination is a central part of the African American experience. It's estimated that every African American experiences about 200 incidents a year, from slurs hurled at them by passing motorists to cashiers who won't put change in their hand, and a whole variety of other unclassifiable events.

This is not the place to go into black history, although it's important to realize that centuries of oppression cannot be quickly eradicated by individual initiative and drive. Its unrealistic to blame African Americans for failing to overcome most barriers because so many of those barriers are deeply rooted in our society. The weight of the past may be the biggest barrier to the future. About 10 million (or 33%

of) African Americans fit the Census Dept. definition of "poor". These poverty rates are extremely stable, and are the same as they were thirty years ago. They show no signs of budging, although there are slight yearly fluctuations.

At a time when white families have increasingly become dual-income units, but this is essentially the same observation as the *Moynihan Report* (1965), which has been largely discredited. Another problem may be employment insecurity. Blacks are over represented in service sector jobs (*McJobs.com*), where employment is less secure. Blacks are also over represented on unemployment and welfare rolls. African Americans are the most segregated group in U.S. society.

There are many ways to measure segregation, but the most common way is to look at housing and residential areas, calculating the amount of ethnic concentration in geographical areas. Blacks are also extremely over represented in city public housing developments. One concern about this problem has to do with health issues. The infant mortality rate for blacks in America is one of the highest in the world, higher than any industrialized country, and higher even than some third world countries. Black children in the 1-4 age range have mortality rates twice that of white children. Black teenagers have mortality rates 10 times that of whites, and homicide is a leading cause of death. Black adults have a mortality rate 30% to 40% more than whites.

The death rates may have something to do with the fact that, percentage-wise, there are fewer blacks now in America than during slavery. It may be useful at this point to take a side journey and explore the ideologies of the black liberation struggle. Many people, blacks included, are often confused about the exact nature of these struggles.

Most of the older leaders were assassinated before they could really articulate their plans, and there have been numerous splits and divisions since then. The most divisive issue has been the question of whether to establish a separate existence or integrate into the dominant culture. Separatism is further divided between tactical separatism and ultimate separatism, with the latter desiring a strictly black state. A concise summary is provided of selected figures that are considered revolutionaries (or criminals to the white establishment): Malcolm X (1925-1965) started the separatist line, the creation of all-black communities, all-black institutions, and internationalization of the struggle. Martin Luther King (1929-1968) stressed the integrationist line, speaking of a time when little black boys and black girls will be able to join hands with little white boys and white girls as sisters and brothers.

Booker T. Washington (1856-1915) stressed acculturation and adaptation to existing realities. W.E.B. Dubois (1868-1963) stressed the need for more government involvement in changing economic conditions, which exploited blacks. Marcus Garvey (1880-1940) endorsed the "Back to Africa" movement. Stokely Carmichael, H. Rap Brown, and Angela Davis (circa 1964) led the "Black Power" movement, which was basically socialist and saw capitalism as the major problem. The "Black Muslim" movement, led by Elijah Muhammad and his more moderate son, W.D. Muhammad, also about this time desired racial separatism, and came to believe that white people were devils created by a black scientist named

Yakub, and Allah was so upset with Yakub, Allah ordained that white people shall rule blacks for a fixed amount of time, although this ideology is more closely associated with a splinter group called the "Five Per Centers".

The "Black Panther" movement (circa 1966) was led by Huey Newton, Bobby Seale, and Fred Hampton as a paramilitary, self-defense group which included the goal of overthrowing capitalism, but the Party split in 1971 under Eldredge Cleaver who advocated providing services to black communities. The modern Black Panthers aim is to expose blacks who sell-out. The NAACP is a justice organization basically pursuing an assimilations approach, patterning routes to success after more model minorities (Asians). The National Urban League is basically a government watchdog group that supports the idea of more rational government programs. Jesse Jackson Jr. basically embraces the unified people of color movement and its fight against neo-colonialism.

The modern Black Muslim movement, called the Nation of Islam, is led by Louis Farrakhan and is basically a racial superiority group for self-betterment, but has also been involved in anti-Zionism. The modern revolutionary struggle, with its Pan-Africanism and Black Nationalist thrusts, is called Kammaasi, and includes groups such as the All-African People's Revolutionary Party (AAPRP) and the Africa Reparations Movement (ARM) which reach out to all Diaspora groups deprived of land, such as the Native Americans, Palestinians, and the Irish. Some of these groups are affiliated with the Communist Party, but some are not. The contemporary struggle is primarily taking place on college campuses with black student associations.

II. *Social Class Discrimination*

African Americans exist at all levels of the American class structure, even the upper-upper class (the "black elite"). There are about 500 incredibly wealthy and politically influential blacks in this country, almost all of them coming from wealthy families that have been so since receiving inheritances from the days of slavery. Persons such as Senator Edward Brooke and Justice Thurgood Marshall are examples. This group does not tend to associate with other blacks. Their only ties may be through the NAACP or the Urban League. At the lower-upper level (the new rich), about 1500 black entertainers or athletes have achieved wealth and prestige by being lucky or talented. Persons such as Bill Cosby and Michael Jordan are examples. What is unique about this group is that they have done it in one generation. They have faced difficult white stereotyping and insensitivity.

The black middle class (the "black bourgeoisie") is growing. Families in this group are usually small, stable, and well planned. In most respects, they are like white middle class families. Studies on this group have shown that they compensate for financial insecurity at times with conspicuous consumption, but that is also something that whites do.

Like whites, this group is stuck in the middle; too well-off to qualify for most tax breaks and too far in debt to ever get out of it on their own. At this level, you also begin to notice the shortage of black males able to support a nuclear family, and there have been numerous examples of one-parent households making it to middle-class status.

An estimated two-thirds of all African Americans fall into the lower classes, and as indicated previously, one-third is below the poverty line. The majority, then, are in the upper-lower ("working" or "proletariat") class. Typical occupations include truck driving, industrial jobs, construction, or auto mechanics. They value hard work, a college education, and a better life for their children. They have faced color barriers preventing them from getting ahead. Blacks at the lower-lower level are completely powerless, alienated, disorganized, segregated, in despair, and have no hopes of getting ahead. They have a disproportionate number of contacts with social workers and police officers. They have become society's scapegoat for the taxpayer's frustrations. *The most important point in under-standing discrimination against African Americans is to realize that the lower-lower class black has become the stereotype of all blacks in America.* Failure to recognize this is called social class discrimination.

III. *Lifestyle Discrimination*

The origin of blacks in America is the only continent in the world with practices that are completely dissimilar to anything Euro centric. It's not that they didn't develop any law, science, or social institutions; it's just that they developed completely different ones that few anthropologists could understand. Further, each one came from a different tribe, with their own language, genetics, and customs. Therefore, when we talk about the existence of a popular "black culture", like the one portrayed by hip-hop music, it's just amazing that anything could cohere these diverse peoples around a common culture. Yet it is well recognized that a black culture exists, with unique demeanor, speech, clothing, and food.

Lifestyle Discrimination is based on the idea that black culture is somehow inferior, which is impossible since cultures are neither inferior nor superior, but rather, functional in terms of survival value for its people. The history of this idea may very well be as a fallback position from the discredited idea of biological inferiority. Alternatively, it may envy at how well some elements of black culture have penetrated white culture.

Much has been made of the legacy of slavery as a central element in black culture. The phrase "legacy of slavery" means neo-colonialism, which means modern or new forms of dominating paternalism. In criminal justice, the equivalent phrase is "seeing the police as an occupying army". The thinking operates on the basis of analogy; e.g., most blacks are kept in slum dwellings, usually owned by white absentee landlords; there are no community services unless they serve the needs of the community with cheap labor; and specially trained police are ready to seal off the area and quell any disturbance.

The situation is analogous to: the colonists are provided the means for rudimentary shelter and they will get more when they start contributing to the commonwealth but meanwhile, our army stands ready to crackdown on the slightest sign of insurrection.

It's not called colonialism because the people involved are citizens, not colonists. *It's called neo-colonialism and it's built into our institutional structure.*

IV. *Skin Color Discrimination*

As the most visible minority group in America, African Americans stand out. Although skin color is genetic, in a sociological sense it's a master status. The prejudice comes easy because black and white are instantly perceived as opposite colors. The problem comes in when characteristics like visible skin color are taken as indicators of quality, quality of housing, quality of service, quality of product, etc. Whether we're talking about neighborhoods, restaurants, swimming pools, or department stores, there's always the suspicion that "the grass is greener on the other side". Whites automatically suspect inferior quality wherever black-skinned faces are found, and blacks automatically suspect superior quality wherever white-skinned faces are found. It's more than just product placement, marketing, and consumer habit. It's our common law.

The most important legal case in African American history is ***Plessy v. Ferguson***, an 1896 Supreme Court decision that upheld the constitution-ality of a Louisiana statute requiring white and "colored" persons to be furnished "separate but equal" accommodations on railway trains. Now, most people know that the "separate but equal" doctrine was overturned in 1954 with ***Brown v. Board of Education,*** but *Plessy* is instructive in the sense that it dealt with the whole matter of race relations while

Brown is mainly about education only. Let's take a short look at the reasoning behind the majority opinion in this case: *(Justice Henry Billings Brown speaking)* "Facilities need not be identical to be equal, and if blacks see what they are provided with as inferior, it's not by reason of anything found in what they are provided with, but solely because they have chosen to put that construction on it." *(Plessy v. Ferguson 1896).*

What do you think this means? I think it means, despite the overturning in **Brown** that blacks are forever deprived of their right to exercise intuition and preference about the quality of things that whites are provided with. This is nothing less than the worst kind of apartheid, a policy of racial discrimination that denies one group the whole freedom to choose what is good and what is bad. We have a similar tradition in criminal justice with our domestic violence problem. Feminists have argued for years that the victims of domestic violence can tell when its about to happen, but courts, scientists, and police tell them there's no such thing as woman's intuition, and nobody can do anything until the perpetrator makes a move. The point I'm trying to make is that *skin color discrimination is very subtle.*

V. *Economic Discrimination*

African Americans throughout most of the 20th Century have been discriminated against in housing, education, employment, and politics. The FHA, up until just a couple of decades ago, affirmed and supported the placing of restrictive covenants in trust deeds, and the practice of redlining is still suspected of being engaged in by some home mortgage lenders. Separate, inferior school buildings existed for most of the century, and even today, the issue of adequate state support for Historically Black Colleges and Universities (HBCUs) is couched in Proposition 209-type terms that such support will be a drain on public resources. In the industrial job market, which is the primary target for most blacks, the unions either had rules forbidding black membership or leadership.

The political parties and political organizations always had less powerful "auxiliaries" they shuffled their black members off to, even today with "black caucuses". Nowhere and by no one are these past discriminations even recognized or addressed.

The sad condition of poverty among most of the black population is attributed, instead, to a lack of motivation and effort. Affirmative Action, which is the only redress that has been offered, is rapidly becoming dismantled due to its unpopularity and charges of reverse discrimination. Indeed, when politicians say that the proper role of government is not to fix all of

America's socio-economic problems, what they really mean is that there will be no redress for past discriminations against African Americans. Bills to award slavery reparations (sponsored by people like U.S. Representative John Conyers) have been soundly defeated in Congress. On the other hand, there are those blacks (like radio talk show host, Alan Keyes, who are conservative and want to dismantle Affirmative Action. The glass ceiling for blacks is worthy of mention. In the corporate world, they are usually appointed or promoted to human resources or public relations positions, where they serve a "showcase" function to the outside world and can't do any harm internally. The real production, sales, and marketing (revenue stream) positions go to whites, which are "fast tracks" to top management. Black executives also rarely have mentors or networks to support them on a day-to-day basis.

VI. *Criminal Justice Discrimination*

Over time, the African American community has formed certain perceptions about police behavior that represent an overall lack of trust in the criminal justice system. The table shows this lack of trust:

POLICE ACTION:	BLACK PERCEPTION:
Stopping blacks in white neighborhood	Whites want blacks "in their place"
Suspecting blacks as drug dealers	Skin color is basis of probable cause
Use of force against blacks	Blacks must be submissive or else
Talking down to/ interrogating blacks	Officer is a racist
Accidental shootings	Bad attitudes come out under stress

Slow response time

Black-on-black crime doesn't matter

Enforcing local ordinances

Police are pawn of white people

Police sticking together to a story

They're covering up a racist conspiracy

VII. *The State Of Black American Politics*

Dr. Martin Kilson's grand overview of the course of Black American electoral politics during the past three decades is required reading for all persons concerned with U.S. history and politics. Kilson's exposition and interpretation of the core agenda that has mobilized African American activists, politicians and voters, from passage of the Voting Rights Act of 1965 through to what Dr. Kilson calls the current "maturation phase" of electoral activity, will certainly be referenced by scholars and journalists in the decades to come. Kilson, who enjoys a special place among Black America's pre-eminent political scientists, skillfully interprets data compiled by the Joint Center for Political Studies to trace the remarkable commonality of mainstream civil rights organizations' political positions and those championed by African American officeholders.

This struggle around "core issues" - defined by Kilson as "housing, jobs, education, criminal justice, and an overall pro-active federal role in ending racism's impact in these areas" - has served as the practical and authentic nexus of the political conversation between African Americans and those who speak on their behalf.

It is the Republican Party's failure to address the core Black agenda that has led to the GOP's "abysmal" electoral record among African Americans, says Kilson. He notes, however, that "signs of attitudinal fissures" have arisen along generational lines regarding the idea of school vouchers, both among Black officeholders and within the African American electorate.

Kilson points out that "the 'generational-conflict' notion is only applied to black politics" never to Latinos and whites. He sounds a "wake-up call to Black America's national civil rights leadership," to be vigilant in the face of emerging "stealth candidacies" of Black nominal Democrats backed by rightwing money.

First-term Newark city councilman Cory Booker's 2002 effort to oust four-term incumbent Sharpe James was a major manifestation of this threat, says Kilson. He warns of more such "stealth candidacies" to come, "fueled by conservative funding sources linked to the Republican Party." There is no better point of departure for portraying the maturation phase of the political status of African-Americans in the overall American political process than examining this year's 30th Annual Report on Black Elected Officials by the Washington-based think tank, the Joint Center for Political and Economic Studies, and written by its senior political analyst, Dr. David Bositis.

Under the deft leadership of Eddie Williams, the Joint Center has provided the indispensable service of tracking both the growth and overall comparative systemic attributes of African-Americans holding the several kinds of political office in the United States since 1970.

All Americans genuinely interested in the growth of equality and diversity in political office holding in our American democracy is greatly in its debt for having skillfully performed this function for a generation and a half.

An overview of Black Elected Officials as the militant phase of the Civil Rights Movement began to gain a favorable public policy and legislative response from the United States Federal Government by, say, 1964, there were around 350 Black elected officials. When those halcyon days ended and the Joint Center conducted its first census of Black Elected Officials (BEOs) in 1970, that number had reached 1,469.

The steady shift in the politics of African-American life between 1970 and today - from full-fledged civil rights activism to a mixed-politics of both civil rights activism and sophisticated Black electoral mobilization - has produced the unprecedented number of 9,040 BEO's the Joint Center found for the year 2000. This figure amounts to between two percent and three percent of all United States elected officials. Viewed in regional terms, some 869 BEOs, or 9.7 percent of the total represent Northeast states; 1,636, or 18.2 percent, represent Midwest states; and 326, or 3.6 percent represent Western states. Not surprisingly, the South recorded the largest 30-year growth in BEOs, with 6,170, or 68.5 percent of the total. The reasons for this are plain enough. First, about 55 percent of all African Americans live in the South.

Secondly, local, state, city, and federal office holding jurisdictions include large concentrations of African Americans. And thirdly, the necessity of ethnic-bloc political and electoral mobilization is still a reality of African-American life today - just as Irish-American, Jewish-American, Polish-American, Italian-American, Latino-American, Chinese-American, WASP-American, etc. ethnic-bloc political and electoral mobilization are still realities in overall American life. Keep in mind that ever since the rise of an ethnically pluralistic American political culture in the post-Civil War era, when Irish-Catholic Americans became a major force in the urban industrial working class - and were joined from the 1890s onward by Italian-Americans, Polish-Americans, Jewish-Americans, Chinese-Americans, Japanese-Americans, etc. - the American political culture has allowed democratic space for ethnic-bloc political and electoral mobilization.

The WASP host cultural group in our American democracy first designed and utilized electoral methods based on ethnic patterns. WASPS did this initially in the pre-Civil War era with political exclusion purposes in mind; they manipulated voting boundaries or districts to keep down the votes of competing religious groups among the WASP sector. Then, from the post-Civil War era onward, competing WASP politicians also manipulated electoral districts for political inclusion purposes, recruiting Irish Catholic voters who might favor Republican Party candidates in industrial cities or states over Democratic Party candidates. This WASP-initiated manipulation of electoral mobilization through the design and re-design of voting districts became known as "gerry-mandering," after Elbridge Gerry, the 18th-century WASP highborn Massachusetts merchant who had an extraordinary but deeply checkered career in the political life of the young nation.

As governor of Massachusetts in 1811 (Gerry would become James Madison's vice president in 1813, before dying in 1814), it was his party's redrawing of voting districts - one of which had the shape of a salamander - to ensure their continued power that his opponents seized upon to produce the eternal pun... From the 1890s on, as Irish-Americans learned to employ ethnic-bloc activism in the electoral process, such ethnic-bloc patterns became a key element in expanding the political incorporation of weak and marginal white groups. It was through such democratic ethnic-bloc electoral space that the first Irish-American city councilmen, mayors, state assemblymen, congressmen, and governors gained office in great states and cities like New York and New York City, Illinois and Chicago.

Finally, the names of James Michael Curley (an early Irish Mayor in Boston and also Governor in Massachusetts), Timothy Sullivan (an early Irish Mayor in New York City), Alfred Smith (first Irish governor of New York and in 1928 the first Irish candidate for president of the United States), and even John Fitzgerald Kennedy (in 1960 the first victorious Irish candidate for president) reflect the long-standing pragmatic weaving of ethnic-bloc modalities into the electoral fabric of American political culture.

VIII. *Racism Among Some Jewish Intellectuals*

No, this is not an anti-Semitic book or an unjustified attack on anyone. It is an attempt to clarify what's going on with African American demands for reparations for slavery and its aftermath, the attacks from David Horowitz, Elie Weisel and The Holocaust Corporation. This book also examines why Philip Roth in his novel, The Thurman Stain, likens African Americans to apes and why John Entine is bringing up that old African American athletes are what they are and excel because of their genetic breeding (something akin to Hitler's attack on African Americans after the German Olympics of 1936). And, why it is that the U.S. media is taking a hands-off approach to these dastardly and inhumane racial slurs? Why are such writers as Roth, Weisel, Entine and other Jews suddenly turning into racists? Or have they always been racists but until now been afraid to come out in the public with it? Do they think that by attacking African Americans that the other white supremacists will forget about them and focus on African Americans, Farrakhan, Latinos and Arabs and let them alone? Perhaps!

On the other hand, there are Jewish writers such as Anthony Lewis, Steve Kowit and Naom Chomsky who want nothing to do with this new Nazi-ism of some of their fellow Jews. Shelby Foote, who passed himself off as a plain white southerner, has now made it plain that he is a Jew, which is fine; but I, and I'm sure others, were shocked when he likened the Ku Klux Klan to the French Resistance of WW II!

Scott Simon of NPR recently inferred that though Daniel Boone and others, who were anti-Mexican racists and the spiritual children of Cortez, at the Alamo, should be admired because they followed their principles and their orders; doesn't this sound like the Jews should have admired the SS troops who killed them because they believed in their principles? Have these men such as Roth, Horowitz, Simon, Entine and Weisel lost their minds? Or are they just echoing a long felt feeling that may have pervaded many Jews that blacks according to Schwartz were and still are inferior to God's chosen people? Perhaps the rise of white supremacists has allowed these men to join the other white men in condemning and attacking African Americans. First, let us understand that over 5 times as many African Americans died in the American slave trade as died in the Holocaust. But let it also be known that among those millions executed, many were not Jews but were Poles, Russians, other Slavic peoples and French, Catholics, Protestants and atheists.

The Holocaust that happened against Africans who were the forefathers of our present African Americans, the indigenous Americans, also called the Native Americans, Amery-Indians, etc., and the driving out of 8 million Palestinians from their homes and their continued brutality at the hands of Israel, should not be called holocausts because the Jewish Holocaust Corporation has deemed only Jews could suffer a holocaust. Not only that, but if anyone raises a question about this Holocaust Corporation or against Israel or any Jewish writer, they are called anti-Semites.

This is another distortion of the language and of truth. Thus, not only has this Holocaust Corporation usurped the term Holocaust for them exclusively, but they also have misrepresented the linguistic definition of Semitic. Actually, Semitic is a language group, not a racial group. In fact, if there is an original group, it's the Abyssinians who were speaking Amharic before there was a Hebrew language.

At that time there were the Aramaic speakers, who were Arabs and people like Abraham, and then Jews came at about the same time as Arabic and Hebrew. This in essence, is the Semitic languages. Therefore, the languages of Aramaic, Amharic Arabic and Hebrew are not for the Jewish community alone. Also, for the sake of accuracy, Abraham spoke Aramaic, not Hebrew. So much for Hebrew being God's language! Now we come to David Horowitz and his ad in the Brown University Student Newspaper in which he gave his reasons for denying reparations to African Americans. In his allegations, he did not address any of the real reasons that African Americans sought reparations namely, the destruction of large families who were brought to America as slaves and then split up. The deaths of so many during the passage to America, the years of slavery and brutality visited upon African Americans. Then, the aftermath of slavery which was harmful discrimination that went on, and continues to this day in the workplace, in social areas, in the media, in educational testing, and in educational and professional profiling against African Americans (through red-lining of loans, through racial profiling by police, through discrimination in court decisions, etc.).

If Jewish survivors of the Hitlerian Holocaust should be compensated, Japanese Americans compensated, Native Americans compensated, why not African Americans who's suffering was much longer, more devastating, and more cruel than the other ethnic groups who were compensated? Horowitz never answers this question in his attacks on African Americans and their quest for compensation. Incidentally, though he cries about the Holocaust, Horowitz never sheds one tear for the suffering of the Palestinians whose land was taken for his Holocaust survivors to create Israel. Weisel, Roth, Horowitz all use double standards in their moral judgments; thus, from their writings, it appears that they believe that anyone who is not a Jew should be seen as inferior (except for the White Supremacists who scare the hell out of most decent Jews, and maybe even Weisel and company).

But, since most of the media is owned by Zionist leading owners, some of these media moguls of venom and hatred, like Horowitz, Weisel and other pro-Zionist columnists will continue to have their way with little opposition allowed in the mass media because of the Zionist control the media. Sarnoff of NBC, Paley of CBS, Goldensohn of ABC and friendly of NPR, and the families that own and control the NY Times and The Washington Post were, and are, strongly pro-Zionist, and in most cases were of Ashkenazim backgrounds (so they had little cultural understanding for the Sephardic Jews or Arabs who actually populated the Middle East and Palestine for the past 3000 years). Why is it that Elie Weisel, who won a Nobel Prize for his Humanitarian work, has been at the forefront of stopping African Americans and Palestinians from claiming their just place as Holocaust victims?

The phrase "Never Again" is the motto of the Holocaust Museum and is supposed to be for mankind but somehow, it pertains only to Jews and to the Holocaust Corporation and its supporters. So we ask how hollow is Never Again? If it applies only to one ethnic group, when suffering is more widespread and allegedly this museum was to be a boon to mankind, not just for those who suffered in the Holocaust. But then again, history is strange. Often the poor whites in the south were more cruel to the blacks than the wealthier whites, because these poor whites identified with the richer and more prominent whites and they felt they were carrying out their wishes because of the southern rhetoric used by so many of the wealthier southern whites. This does not excuse the wealthier whites, even to this day. Sadly enough, Ted Turner had a message at Thanksgiving some years back at the Atlanta Airport to the effect that he missed the days of My Old Kentucky Home? And he has had the music from Gone With The Wind played as a memento to the Old south, two insults to African Americans. It is the same when you turn on NPR programs; it has become the Shelby Foote, Ken Burns's view of history assisted by Gates. I saw the documentary about Gen. Stonewall Jackson, and it was so overloaded with sentiment that I almost forgot that Jackson was fighting to defend slavery!

It is clear that NPR is not for all of us, but for a chosen few such as Scott Simon, Shelby Foote, Ken Burns, and Daniel Shorr. Where are the African

Americans, the Arab Americans, the Latino Americans, and the Native Americans on the daily and weekly shows? Certainly, we have many trained in journalism and broadcasting, but we cannot break the monopoly; not even for commentary or those little ditties that complain about the world of pots and pans and about how I lost my virginity at 17. There are more important issues to deal with in racism in jazz, racism in politics, racism in education and testing, and so much more--but these weaklings chuckle it off as, "we need a little humor", which is true, but then again, they are supposed to be news not entertainment. Also, why is it that they don't have an African American speaking about racism in Africa or an Arab also reporting on the problems between Palestinians and Israel (why do 90% of these reporters just happen to be Jewish?) Certainly, there must be some other qualified, educated broadcasters in America. Whether it is Salon.com, which features Horowitz and his ilk, NBC, Harpers, NY Times, NPR, it's all the same, politics by Scott Simon and Daniel Shorr on weekends, the freedom of speech often of hate-mongers or politicians from the far right, followed by some tepid centrists allowed to allegedly "balance things out." While those of us who could truly balance things out are kept off the air.

As one commentator put it, "the elitists in the U.S. media see blacks and Arabs as the same", it's just that the Arabs are "sand-niggers and the blacks are jungle-niggers." If they didn't see it this way, why would they treat our people and our concerns as badly as they do? *Freedom of Speech!* Ah, that's an interesting idea, one that's preached about continually in the media when they want to have their position heard--but if you disagree with the editorial position of a television on newspapers outlet--you'll rarely, if ever, be heard from. Yes, you may have freedom to speak your mind, but you certainly won't get heard through the major media because they won't put you on the air or allow your material to be printed in their pages. The problem is much like that in Animal Farm by George Orwell, "some are more equal than others."

This group, that includes people like Horowitz, Weisel, Fox of the B'nai Brith, Roth, Entine, are "more equal" than the rest of us. As one scholar put it, "Do you think the NY Times would ever run an anti-Holocaust compensation ad? But you know they'd run one that was against compensation for African Americans." Do you think they'd run an ad showing Israeli atrocities against Palestinian children and their funerals? Let's get serious; freedom of speech is a ploy to protect those who are in power against those who disagree with them; it keeps them in power over the rest of us who have no major media power. Major media power is what gives you political power in the world. The Lutherans point out that there are "sins of commission and sins of omission." These major media outlets and their lackeys, the Horowitz', Weisel's etc. commit, and the rest are excluded. Thus, they are guilty of the sin of omission by not allowing our voices to be published or heard.

Thus, they are the ones who are destroying the true intent of the U.S. Constitution and Bill of Rights that speaks of "Freedom of Speech;" just as the southerners have always ignored the Bill of Rights and basic Christianity when it came to blacks by not allowing them to be seen as a full human being! The other problem we face in the U.S. at this time is that there aren't many Helen Thomas' or Mike Wallace's or Lowell Bermann's around and most of the current crop of journalists don't have the guts to really go after injustices. Instead, they'd rather be invited to a politician's dinner table, as is the case with so many Washington correspondents, play tennis with the president, as was the case with several TV correspondents, or be invited "down to the ranch" as is going on now with the Bush administration. Martin Luther King, Schwerner, Goodman and all those black and white must be turning over in their graves at this time with this new racism that is flourishing in America.

It is not just from those who speak with racist tones, but also those who keep the true voices out of circulation in the mass media--why weren't there more real jazz musicians on Ken Burns' show, why Stanley Crouch and not Ahmad Jamal or Oscar Peterson or Ishmael Reed--why so much of that Gatesian type musician, Wynton Marsalis; every good trumpet player knows that Wynton is fantastic technically, but that he can't even blow in the same room as Wallace Rooney on trumpet or his brother Branford on sax. So whether it's politics unmasked, or politics as covered in cultural shows by exclusion, it is the same. Thus, it was just that reason that the U.S. was kicked off the UN Human Rights Commission and even kicked off the UN Narcotics Control Commission (because we've been remiss in both areas).

I have often been embarrassed when America has chided and criticized other nations for their racial and human rights violations--because, though we may not be as bad as some, we are no angels in our behavior toward our minorities and we often turn one minority against another in order to allow the ruling group to stay in power; this is often done through the media. In the present situation, the rights of African Americans to have compensation for their years of suffering, past and present, has been given short shrift by the media and many of its leading spokesmen have even spoken against these just reparations. It is doubly sad that so many of these spokesmen are Jewish, they use Hitler's methods against African Americans and against Palestinians and excuse it by saying, "we've suffered--don't tell me about your suffering because it's not as bad." bah, humbug. As they used to say in the 60s, **"IT IS TIME."**

IX. *African American-Jewish Relations*

As priorities in agendas between the African American and Jewish communities have taken each in somewhat divergent directions and as differences over some issues continue, both communities will be challenged to work together to address tensions that might arise as a result of these differences. Increased tensions among many ethnic groups continue. Disadvantaged communities remain without real opportunities and ladders to escape from poverty, and they continue to face ongoing prejudice. Government intervention and private efforts are needed immediately to tackle these evolving problems.

The Jewish and African American communities across the country have on the whole enjoyed positive collaborative relationships that have enabled them to work together particularly on issues of mutual concern. Whether it was joint efforts to see the enactment of civil rights legislation, the enforcement of policies protecting the rights and liberties of all people, or efforts to fight racism, anti-Semitism and bigotry, or even the struggle for improved economic conditions, equal opportunity and access for all people, these two communities have been at the foundation of coalitional endeavors on behalf of these issues. The relationship between the Jewish and African American communities is a complex one containing elements of tension, cooperation, indiffer-ence, contradictory, strong and weak ties, and great expectations.

It is a relationship that can best be appreciated in the context of the respective historical journey of each community in the United States, as these experiences have essentially directed our collective behavior and shaped the attitudes and expectations of one another. This relationship has been intertwined for decades, each having been at some point discriminated against by the larger society, though not to the same extent, in the United States. Oppression of Jews occurred more outside the borders of the U.S., whereas for most African Americans entry into the U.S. marked their enslavement. The Jewish experience in America has included the denial for some of admission to the United States followed by tough working and economic conditions, discrimination and exclusion. However, it also has been a history of having overcome those obstacles and having integrated successfully into the larger society.

This was accomplished, in part, through a vigorous effort by the Jewish community to see the enactment of anti-discrimination legislation that assured the right of all Americans to participate fully and equally in all aspects of society. Such efforts provided the opportunity to join in common cause with African Americans and others who were targets of discrimination.

As the economic status of Jews improved, many in the community moved to the suburbs and became absorbed with middle class and suburban concerns while continuing to hold the same views on public policy issues as African Americans. Jewish concern about the well-being of Israel intensified following the

1967 Six Day War and resulted in intensified advocacy efforts and activities relating to Israel. This combined with concern about the security of Jews in the former Soviet Union and elsewhere resulted in a diminished focus on the domestic agenda. From the outset the black experience in America included slavery, oppression, segregation and institutional racism. When blacks migrated north and west between 1910 and 1950, discrimination often prevented them from getting jobs.

In the 1930s, American blacks were hit hard by the Depression, emerging from it to find them in competition with Latino and Asian immigrants for unskilled jobs, which continued as waves of new immigrants entered the U.S. The passage of legislation outlawing discrimination dramatically increased opportunities for African Americans and others. Notwithstanding these victories, progress continued to be slow as discrimination persisted through attitudes, behavior and sometimes from the failure to enforce the law.

Public opinion began to change in the 1980s regarding society's obligation to redress past discrimination. Some whites that charged reverse discrimination challenged Affirmative Action policies. This also occurred at a time when the economy was in recession, jobs dried up and money was tight.

Tensions increased among various ethnic groups as resentment grew over jobs, resources and perceptions that one group was more favorably treated than another. These tensions also included the African American and Jewish communities in some parts of the country. Moreover, these two communities no longer had the same priority concerns and did not share the same opportunities and successes in the United States. They also held different views on a range of issues, including some Affirmative Action policies, and the response of black leadership to demagogues such as Muslim Minister Louis Farrakhan and others. Within the Jewish community, there were some who believed that the black community had turned its back on the Jewish community by drawing inward, failing to recognize Jewish involvement in the civil rights movement and making erroneous assertions about Jewish positions on affirmative action and other issues. Some American Jews were distressed by the lack of forthright support expressed by some of the grass roots leaders in the African American community towards Israel.

For some it appears to be the failure of many black leaders to condemn expressions of anti-Semitism by such racial polarizes as Louis Farrakhan, Leonard Jeffries, and others also expressed resentment. That concern intensified following the meeting between Louis Farrakhan and the Congressional Black Caucus (CBC) in September 1993, particularly given the strong relationship that has historically existed between the CBC and the Jewish community. In subsequent meetings with CBC members, strong assurances were given that the meeting with Farrakhan did not signal a movement away from the Jewish community. Members of the CBC heard the Jewish community's serious concern regarding the inclusion of Farrakhan in coalitional activities given his unequivocal anti-Semitic, anti-white and other prejudiced comments directed at women and gays.

In a subsequent development, on November 23,

1993, Khalid Abdul Muhammad, a spokesman for the Nation of Islam, delivered an inflammatory speech at Kean College in New Jersey, in which he attacked Jews and whites in general as well as a number of ethnic, religious and other minority groups. The address received widespread public attention as a result of an advertisement placed in The New York Times and elsewhere by the Anti-Defamation League. The ad consisted entirely of excerpts from Muhammad's speech. As a result of this publicity, prominent African American leaders, who called upon Farrakhan to explain the actions of his spokesman, condemned the speech in strong public statements.

Instead of rebuking Muhammad, in a February 3, 1994 press conference Farrakhan denounced the manner in which Muhammad spoke, but said that he stood by "the truth" of what his spokesman had said. Further, he denounced the ADL and called upon African American leaders to distance themselves from that organization. Because of this uneasy alliance between the CBC and the Nation of Islam, African American political leaders' power began to wane. For example, the defeat of Congresswoman Cynthia McKinney of the 4th District of Georgia by Judge Denise Majette has caused vast soul searching among African Americans. We may quibble over the causes of McKinney's defeat. Yes, there was a low Black voter turnout.
Yes, White Republicans crossed over and voted against McKinney in the Democratic primary. Yes, certain prominent African Americans withdrew their support for McKinney at a critical stage before the election. While all of the above were contributing factors to McKinney's defeat, the most significant

43

cause was an outside force that mobilized strong support for her opposition. When asked to identify this force, Georgia state legislator and father of McKinney, Billy McKinney, stated to the media: "J-E-W-S." Indeed, it was the Jewish lobby that not only orchestrated, headed, mobilized and funded Congresswoman McKinney's defeat, these same organized Jews -- particularly the American Israel Public Affairs Committee (AIPAC) also defeated Alabama's five-term Black incumbent, Representative Earl Hilliard, earlier in the year. In McKinney's case, the Jewish lobby raised $1.1 million for Denise Majette -- $500,000.00 more than McKinney had in her war chest.

By stirring up anti-McKinney sentiment in the local and national media and on the internet - depicting her as racist, pro-Arab and militant - the Jewish lobby frightened many White Republicans into voting in a Democratic primary that they would ordinarily have ignored. Further, by exercising their age-old pressure tactics against Black leaders-threatening economic and political reprisals - the Jewish lobby forced them to withdraw their decades-old support for McKinney. How else do we explain why NAACP chairman Julian Bond, Democrat John Lewis of Georgia's neighboring 5th District, former Atlanta Mayor Maynard Jackson and Andrew Young, former Atlanta Mayor and U. S. Ambassador to the U.N., all maintained a conspicuous distance from McKinney during the critical period preceding the election? Following the election, several prominent Jews applauded McKinney's defeat. They claimed that she was too radical, too critical of Israel and too supportive of Arab causes.

While I share the outrage of many African Americans over this, the latest successful move by prominent Jews to silence outspoken Black leaders and to set the Black agenda, I also sense that there is greater indignation now than ever before over this ongoing affront. So much so that for many African Americans this is indeed the last straw!

Consequently, it is high time -- no, long past time -- that African Americans everywhere re-evaluate the so-called Black/Jewish alliance. Some of our leaders, writers and thinkers have already rushed forward to pursue the normal Black course of action during times of crises between Blacks and Jews. For example, the Rev. Jesse Jackson is talking about healing the current rift so as not to endanger this important liberal, democratic alliance.

Furthermore, Professor Ron Walters has written a widely syndicated column that, in essence, minimizes the overarching impact of the Jewish lobby in McKinney and Hilliard's defeats.

Walters focuses on collateral issues that, without the influence of the Jewish lobby, would have been as inconsequential in this election as they have been in the past. This tendency of prominent African Americans to placate Jews by ignoring their excesses or deflecting criticism from them is precisely why so many Jewish leaders and organizations have consistently criticized, defamed, degraded and defeated certain Black leaders with impunity - AND WILL DO SO AGAIN. Jewish leaders have clearly decided that, no matter how widespread the outrage among Black people, if Black leaders - fearing Jewish reprisals- continue to cower before them, to rationalize their racism and to apologize for their flagrant disrespect for African Americans, Jews will suffer no consequences for their actions. History teaches us that

Jews are not the allies that so many African Americans think they have been. It is now widely known that Jews were as much involved in the African slave trade as Arabs and Christians.

Prior to the Civil Rights movement, Jews as a whole in the North and South were no more outspoken against racism, segregation and discrimination than White Christians. Even during the Civil Rights Movement (which benefited Jews far more than African Americans), Dr. King's *"Letter From A Birmingham Jail"* was directed as much toward Jewish Rabbis as toward White ministers, because Jews were generally no more sympathetic to the Black Cause than were White Christians in Alabama.

Over the past thirty years, Jewish racism against Black people has grown exponentially. Whenever a Black leader has spoken out against Israel, criticized Jews or otherwise failed to comply with certain Jewish demands or opinions, organized Jews has mounted a relentless campaign to destroy him. For decades, Israel was South Africa's staunchest ally, while American Jews tacitly endorsed this alliance.

Furthermore, in spite of the fact that Black people everywhere have consistently sympathized with Jewish calls for recompense for their suffering during the Holocaust, many Jewish leaders and organizations have fervently opposed Affirmative Action for Africans Americans and, incredibly, now prominent Jews, like David Horowitz, of the Center For The Study of Popular Culture, and journalist Richard Poe, are at the forefront of the attack against the African American Movement in support of reparations.

Now, in the 21st Century, powerful Jews have also targeted Black Congressmen; in spite of the fact that nearly all of the members of the Congressional Black

Caucus have consistently followed their White colleagues in voting in favor of U.S. military and economic support for Israel.

Although the Jewish lobby has succeeded in defeating McKinney and Hilliard, some Jewish leaders are not jubilant over these developments and are eager to meet with prominent African Americans to mend fences. These Jews realize that, at this juncture in their history - more than at any other time - Jews need Blacks more than Blacks need them. After all, some Jews understand that Black people are the traditional American scapegoats who have shielded Jews from bigotry. In light of this, African Americans must now ask what have we received from Jews in return?

The answer is clear: Control of Black organizations, stereotypes in Hollywood, attacks against outspoken Black scholars, like Dr. Leonard Jeffrey's and Dr. Tony Martin, etc. Through it all, however, Black people have remained loyal and sympathetic to Jews.

But the rest of the world is another story. In their quarterly journal "Response", the Los Angeles-based Simon Wiesenthal Center reports rising anti-Semitism in Eastern and Western Europe, the entire Middle East, Asia and Latin American. Furthermore, in the United States, growing numbers of White Christians are, on the Internet and elsewhere, questioning America's blind loyalty to Israel that has insolated the U.S. and increased the threat of terrorism. And, like African Americans, many Whites are deeply disturbed over the Jewish influence in Congress that has also resulted in the silencing and defeat of certain prominent White Congressmen. In light of the crisis before us, Black leaders must close ranks and act on one accord.

The defeat of McKinney and Hilliard are not the work of a disaffected ally, but some who are cold blooded racists who are willing to block Black progress -- no matter what the cost to African Americans in a loss of power and influence - if it conflicts with the overall Jewish agenda. It is high time, at this historical juncture, for African Americans - the long-suffering, ever-obliging buffer between Whites and Jews - to step aside - and let Jews fend for themselves-so that White people will, at long last, stop focusing on Black people and get a good look at some of the American Jews, whose McCarthyistic tactics and stranglehold on Congress threaten to make this country the United States of Israel.

X. Who Is Black?

Although there are a myriad of reason why the one-drop rule has affected so many African Americans I narrowed it down to some of the most glaring causes. First, Homer Plessy was the plaintiff in the 1896 precedent-setting "separate but equal" case of Plessy v. Ferguson. This challenged the Jim Crow statutes that required racially segregated seating on trains in the interstate commerce in the state of Louisiana. The U.S. Supreme Court quickly dispensed with Plessy's contention that because he was only one-eighth Negro and could pass as white he was entitled to ride the seats reserved for whites. He quickly discovered that without ruling directly on the definition of a Negro, the Supreme Court briefly took what is called the judicial notice of what it assumed to be common knowledge: that a Negro or black is any person with any black ancestry.

Federal courts have thus taken the *judicial notice* of the customary boundary between two sociocultural groups that differ, on the average, in physical traits, not between two discrete genetic categories.

In the absence of proof of a specific black ancestor, the courts have usually accepted merely being known as a black in the community as evidence of black ancestry.

State courts have generally upheld the one-drop-rule. For example, persons in Virginia who are one-fourth or more Indian and less than one-sixteenth African black are defined as Indians as long as they stay on the reservation, but black if they leave.

Up until 1970, a Louisiana statute had embraced the one-drop-rule, defining a Negro as anyone with a trace of black ancestry. They defined a Negro or someone black whose ancestry is more than one thirty-second black.

Another stumbling block that African Americans had to endure because of the one-drop-rule was the Census Enumeration of African Americans. When the U.S. Bureau of the Census enumerates African Americans (counted as Negroes until 1980. Are you kidding me?), it did not use a scientific definition, but rather the one accepted by the general rule public and by the courts.

The definition of black used by the Census Bureau has been the nation's cultural and legal definition: all persons with any known black ancestry. Other nations define and count black differently so international comparisons of census data on blacks can be extremely misleading. Not only does the one-drop rule apply to no other group than African American, but also apparently the rule is unique in that it is found only in the United States and not in any other nation in the world. In fact, definitions of who is black vary quite sharply from country to country.

Finally, in the United States there are still complex, major issues about the opportunities and rights of blacks, but none concerning how we define who is black. The personnel officer, the census taker, the judge, the school admissions staff, the affirmative action officer, and the black political caucus leader all readily classify a predominantly white mulatto... as a black person. The one-drop rule...what a way to keep tabs on a race of people no matter what color they are.

Well thanks to the one-drop rule it has shown just about every ethnic group (America's melting pot) in the U.S. has a trace of African ancestry. Unfortunately, other ethnic groups refuse to accept this discovery and in essence the one-drop rule is to target the African who is a mulatto or some one who is white but earlier stated has African ancestry in their genes. The one-drop rule in the U.S. was created to keep the African on the outside of the "American Dream".

On the other hand, definitions of black vary from country to country. In a Writers and Artist Conference in Paris for example, James Baldwin one of the most celebrated writers at any time was asked by the French Chairperson why did he consider himself a Negro, since he certainly did not look like one. The black experience with passing as white in the United States contrast with the experiences of other ethnic minorities in other countries because a person who is one-fourth or less American Indian or Korean or Filipino is not regarded as passing if he or she intermarries and joins fully the life of the dominant community, so the minority ancestry is not hidden.

Just like in the U.S. however, some ethnic groups in other countries are not accepted into mainstream society by either of the parent groups (unmixed original race groups) they are therefore defined as a totally different and lowly people. For example, mulattoes among the Ganda peoples of Uganda, East Africa are regarded with condescension and contempt by the Ganda as well as not accepted by white society either.

The plan to solve the problem was to move the mulattoes to an island in Lake Victoria, where they would be completely isolated (Oh yeah! sounds just like the U.S. treatment of the African slave and the African American of 1920's-present day).

There is also a similar status position for the Metis in Canada, the Anglo-Indians in India, and Korean-Americans in Korea and Vietnamese-Americans in Vietnam. South Africa's Apartheid is an example of keeping an ethnic group in "its place" that mirrors the U.S. philosophy (former and present-day). The ultimate goal of Apartheid has been to restrict all blacks that are not employed in the Republic native reservations called the Bantustans or Homelands, which comprise less than 14 percent of the country's land although blacks make up more than 70 percent of the population.

Whites in South Africa (like the U.S.) occupy all the good farms and pasture land, and the mines, while Bantustans are discontinuous wastelands with very few resources, no industrial cities, and no seaports. The tribal people are dependent on a money income, yet there is almost no work on the reservations.

Apartheid, pales to the U.S. philosophy, in that its strategy is to present the Homelands to the world as if they were politically independent and to use the cheap native labor in the industrial cities, the mines and on white farms.

The Homelands remain politically and economically dependent on the Republic of South Africa, in which at one point in time they had no vote. In Brazil and other countries in lowland Latin America and the West Indies, the Mestizos and mulattoes originally were buffer groups between whites, unmixed blacks and Indians. Once again paling in comparison to the way the U.S. treats its minorities.

A type of status is occupied by racially mixed Americans who are partly descended from Japanese Americans, American Indians or any other racially visible minorities with the exception of blacks is the status of assimilation.

The one-drop rule and the related concept of passing as white pertains only to blacks in the United States, and the American status rule for mulattoes is also very different from the rules for racially mixed persons...in other places and times.

In summary, the one-drop rule verifies what many scholars throughout the world over the last several centuries have known but was afraid to admit. Africans encompass the world and many (if not all) ethnic groups throughout the world are in earnest affected by the one-drop rule. An area that has been shrouded in secrecy and misinformation has been the status of the mulattoes who had always been considered a white Negro because of their color. It was believed that mulattoes relationship with Caucasians in America and abroad were on some-what good terms towards one another.

But the mulatto's relationships between the other African Americans were sour because it was felt mulattoes had turned their back on their "race" by trying to pass as white.

On the contrary, however, while this might have been true of some mulattoes turning their back on their race, only a small number of them had engaged in these selfish acts of betrayal. On the other hand, many mulattoes used their skin color to their advantage to aid the rest of the African American community.

An example of this bravery was Walter White former president of the NAACP who risks life on a daily basis to go down south and expose the coward acts of lynching and burning African American for no reason except for being *African American*.

The issue of Miscegenation has been quite murky for sometime now.

Scholars have dealt with this subject over the years with "kid gloves" if you will. They presented to the public in their books, and lectures that Miscegenation were isolated incidents and that no decent, law abiding, good natured Caucasian (especially Southerners) would ever engage in such a vile act. Once again, the truth is exposed. More Southerners (Caucasian men and women alike) did in fact engage in this act that many considered a "stain" on the very essence of America.

There was a time when my relationship with other ethnic groups was very good in particular the Puerto Rican community. My neighborhood as a child was a "melting pot" of African American, Puerto Ricans, as well as Caucasians of different ethnic backgrounds. We not only were cordial and respectful to each other cultures and heritage, we also assisted one another when it called for it. No family in the neighborhood went hungry because each ethnic group treated one another like a close family relative.

I saw this peace accord between different cultures through the eyes of a child. Unfortunately, once I grew up and left my country (my neighborhood) I experienced some of the most blatant racism that one could experience.

Let me be candid! It was not just the W.A.S.P. (White, Anglo, and Saxon Protestant) and Jewish communities who engaged in racist ideology about African Americans. No!

It was also by the Asian and Puerto Rican communities alike who engaged in the same rhetoric as the other ethnic groups I have mentioned.

Unfortunately, I went out into the world with "blinders' on. In essence, I was colorblind and society changed that perception expeditiously. Today, my relationships with other ethnic groups are "strained" at the very least.

Betrayal, hypocrisy, and arrogance on behalf of the aforementioned have jaded my views and ideology about the other ethnic groups' cultures and heritage. Finally, perhaps Davis said more than he knew in his magnificent work and at the same time opened up old wounds that other ethnic groups were not ready to hear or accept...all of us are in fact are of the same race.

Here is a quote from Mr. Davis's Who Is Black? The things that make us different are how we think. What we believe is to be important and the way we look at life. It does not matter if you go by race or ethnicity because America (and now the rest of the world, thanks to America) you are not judged by your individuality, but the color of your skin. As a proud African American I want to be known as that, yet I still want society to know that I have freethinking views.

Unfortunately, many Americans do not share this concept. From Mr. Davis brilliant work I am able to present the ammunition that proves my theory as to why race relations are so strained in today's society and why conflict between different ethnic groups are at an all time high. In addition, according to Davis's data that it is believed that every ethnic group in the United States is in some way related to the African American. Why? Could it be that five hundred years ago the slave masters of different ethnic groups (Irish, Italian, Spanish, European, etc.) owned slaves and also used them as concubines? Possibly!

Or could it be Miscegenation, the blending of African American and an assortment of other ethnic groups? Absolutely!

I prefer "ethnicity" because it presents the *essence of being apart of a group*, yet still has the *aura of your individuality.* On the other hand, "race" is too stagnant and stiff. It represents that you are apart of a group, but lack individuality. It projects negative stereotypes. For example," we all look alike" or "they all do what he or she (something that is negative) doing. Alas, this is all conjecture because society has a way of prostituting words that are clear and definitive, and "ethnicity" is definitive.

In the end however, using even this term instead of "race" is a blow to ethnic pride. Perhaps in the next twenty years we'll come up with another term to distinguish between our unity as a group and our different views as individuals...but I doubt it.

XI. *Racial Inequality Among Americans*

In 1986, Japanese Prime Minister Yasuhiro Nakasone remarked that the average American intellectual standard is lower than the average Japanese standard because of the blacks and Hispanics in the U.S. He has often said that the source of Japan's strength lies in its "racial homogeneity." Eleven years later, University of Texas Law School Professor Lino Graglia triggered a firestorm of criticism for his remarks that "Blacks and Mexican-Americans are not academically competitive with whites in selective institutions. It is the result primarily of cultural effects. They have a culture that seems not to encourage achievement. Failure is not looked upon with disgrace." It has been said that racism is the plague of civilization. In 1977, Andrew Young, at that time the chief U.S. representative to the United Nations, claimed that a race war in South Africa would inevitably precipitate racial conflict in the United States. Some countries, like Great Britain and Australia, eliminated the potential for conflict by simply denying or severely limiting entry.

However, American society has always been enriched by its waves of immigrants. John Kennedy observed how Alexis de Tocqueville saw the United States as "a society of immigrants, each of whom had begun life anew, on an equal footing". This was the secret of America: a nation of people with the fresh memory of old traditions who dared to explore new frontiers. In 2004, the Census Bureau predicted that in the year 2050 minority groups would comprise one-half of the total American population of 420 million. Hispanics will comprise roughly one-quarter of the population, blacks 15%, and Asians 8%.

As the proportion of Americans increasingly becomes Hispanic, black and Asian, inequalities grow. According to the Pew Hispanic Center's 2004 *"The Wealth of Hispanic Households: 1996 to 2002"* study, "the median net worth of Hispanic households in 2002 was $7,932. This was only nine percent of $88,651, the median wealth of non-Hispanic White households at the same time. The net worth of Non-Hispanic Blacks was only $5,988. Thus, the wealth of Latino and Black households is less than one-tenth the wealth of White households even though Census data show their income is two-thirds again as high. Here we consider some of the sociological facets of race and ethnicity, and how they are interwoven with other dimensions of social stratification.

Ethnicity And Race General Indexes

MINORITY GROUP-A group typically numerically inferior to the rest of the population of a state, in a non-dominant position, whose members--being nationals of the state-- possess ethnic, religious, or linguistic characteristics distinguishing them from the rest of the population. Typically, members of a minority group share a sense of solidarity and a desire to preserve their culture, traditions, religion, or language. A minority group can sometimes be a numerical majority in a minority group position.

Minority group status is not a matter of numbers; it is determined by the presence of distinguishing features such as discrimination. Central features character-izing a minority group are:

- The members of a minority group suffer various disadvantages at the hand of another group.

- A minority group is identified by group characteristics that are socially visible.

- People usually do not become members of a minority group voluntarily; they are born into it.

- By choice or necessity, members of a minority group tend to marry within the group."

The "melting pot" which America is referred to, is not really true. Presently, looking at the situation it is more like a non-dissolved liquid. As time goes on racism seems to grow with it.

There have been public issues such as the Rodney King trials and the Crown Heights incident that have increased racism in the country. Racism is a very pressing problem in America. Unfortunately, this is a good example about how our society doesn't change and is very hateful. As people from today's society we are often taught hate, or prejudice.

There are many organizations around that promote this kind of hatred. Almost everyone in there life has experienced a feeling of racism in his or her own mind. Hopefully this will be able to change after education and other methods to teach that there are petty differences between races. Essentially, all races are the same and should be looked upon by everyone as such.

The White Christian Nations and other racist organizations that shroud themselves in religious ideology for example, are groups, which believe in many different things than the Protestant or Catholic religions.

They base their views on the Bible, the true Word of God (Yahweh). They believe that the Bible was written for and about a specific section of people, that people being the white race.

XII. *The Reality of Racism*

Reality has just begun. We live in the greatest nation in the world. Nonetheless, our country is suffering the wrath of a violent cell in our communities that has caused terrorism and played havoc throughout the nation. We fail to recognize the problem and we fail to treat the cause of the problem. We pretend the problems are drugs, welfare, Affirmative Action, and the black community in our inner cities. Media highlights black crime as the only crime. The powerful in America for example, have succeeded in sweeping under the rug the true fact that Rodney King beatings happen every day of the year in every metropolitan city in America.

America is slowly becoming aware that this stereotyping of black people is the hard and honest truth. America is suffering church burnings and other terrorist acts such as the bombing of the Federal Building in Oklahoma City, TWA flight 800, the bombing at the Olympics in Atlanta, and now 9/11.

Remember Susan Smith? She brutally murdered her two little boys and blamed a black man. Also, a white female state trooper in Georgetown, DE, (Dawn R. Frakes), fabricated a story about being shot by a black teenager. Mark Fuhrman is free, having paid a mere $200 fine? Had Fuhrman been a black man, he would be doing time within a month after he lied under oath once his racist beliefs were exposed. A policeman! These people thrive in our society and are protected by the white community. The white society hides behind the term, "isolated incident.

"The media is guilty of these fabrications." Police report the incident to be isolated. It was stated that race played no factor in the bombings. The question must be asked, when are all of the so-called isolated incidents, going to be accepted as an epidemic concerning racial violence in our society?

It is odd that we in the black community are blamed for the violence in our society. Yet we never hear of The Nation of Islam committing these acts! We never hear of the Rainbow Coalition or the NAACP held responsible for any violent act of terrorism. On the contrary, we continue to read and witness Skin Heads, the KKK, Freemen, Neo-Nazi groups and the various white Militias who are white hate groups, who are the violent cell in our society. These weekend warriors practice war games religiously, using black cardboard men as targets. They hide behind religion, secrecy and patriotism, claiming to be good Americans. These groups hold classes and stockpile weapons and explosives. They construct bombs such as the one that exploded at the Atlanta Olympic Games in 1996, and the bombing of the Federal Building in Oklahoma. The Internet is a web-supporting network of white supremacy hates groups. Beware, because their numbers are growing. These acts have gone far beyond job discrimination and black people not being allowed to move next door.

America must recognize first that we do have an enemy from within. We are speaking about a war on bigotry in our society. Are we going to stand by and let our nation self-destruct? America must come together, (both black and white). The time is now. The war is upon us, for both black and white people of this nation.

White America can no longer ignore this growing problem. We have white people who are fearful of speaking up for what is right and just, and who are fearful of their own white brother. Why do you let this minority have power over us? We have the power. Let's use it.

XIII. *U.S. Race Relations Improve, Yet Problems Persist*

A majority of Americans support Affirmative Action believes race relations have improved since the Civil Rights Movement and approve of interracial marriage, according to a new poll. Still, 49% of blacks said they had experienced some form of discrimination in the month preceding the poll and 62% believe they are treated somewhat or very unfairly.

"The good news is there is a sense of optimism in the respondents to the poll. There is a real sense that America has changed for the better," said Wade Henderson, executive director of the Leadership Conference on Civil Rights, a coalition that includes AARP, unions and religious organizations. However, Henderson said, the poll also "shows there is a gulf, not only in perception, but in reality" when it comes to differing views on discrimination.

The Gallup Organization Poll, commissioned by the AARP was released to coincide with the 50th Anniversary of the Brown vs. Board of Education ruling that declared school segregation unconstitutional.

Gallup said it is the organization's most comprehensive survey on race relations. In the poll of adults 18 and older, nearly 90% of whites, 73% of blacks and 76% of Hispanics said race relations had somewhat or greatly improved. Americans of different races are increasingly comfortable living together: 78% of blacks, 61% of Hispanics and 57% of whites said they prefer to live in a mixed neighborhood. Fifty-seven percent of Americans support affirmative action, a finding that Henderson called a pleasant surprise. "Americans in a general manner accept the equitable principle that, for every wrong, there is a remedy," he said.

Sixty-three percent, however, said that "race relations will always be a problem in the U.S." according to Census Bureau projections, whites, now about 69% of the population, would drop to 50.1% by 2050. More than a quarter of those surveyed said that will be a good thing. Fifty-six percent said it will not matter, and 13% said it would be a bad thing. Tyrone Miller, a 47-year-old black man from the Bronx, suggested that behavior has changed, but some attitudes have not. "Minorities are pulling the American economy, so if you really want to make money and get ahead, it's not profitable to be racist," said Miller, a security manager. "But that doesn't mean you'll be invited to that person's home."

Among other findings:

- 73 percent of Americans approve of interracial marriage. In a 1958 Gallup Poll, when the question was posed only to whites, just 4% supported mixed marriages.

- 21 percent of whites said they have been a victim of reverse discrimination.

- 56 percent of whites, 38% of Hispanics and 21% of blacks said all or most of the Civil Rights Movement's goals had been achieved.

XIV. *An Agenda for Peace...Maybe!*

Introduction

1. In its statement of 31 January 1992, adopted at the conclusion of the first meeting held by the Security Council at the level of Heads of State and Government, countries from around the world were invited to prepare, for circulation to the Members of the United Nations by 1 July 1992, an analysis and recommendations on ways of strengthening and making more efficient within the framework and provisions of the Charter the capacity of the United Nations for preventive diplomacy, for peacemaking and for peace-keeping.

2. The United Nations is a gathering of sovereign States and what it can do depends on the common ground that they create between them. The adversarial decades of the Cold War made the original promise of the Organization impossible to fulfill. The January 1992 Summit therefore, represented an unprecedented recommitment, at the highest political level, to the Purposes and Principles of the Charter.

3. In these past months a conviction has grown, among nations large and small, that an opportunity has been regained to achieve the great objectives of the Charter - a United Nations capable of maintaining international peace and security, of securing justice and human rights and of promoting, in the words of the Charter, "social progress and better standards of life in larger freedom". This opportunity must not be squandered. The Organization must never again be crippled as it was in the era that has now passed.

4. It draws upon ideas and proposals transmitted to me by Governments, regional agencies, non-governmental organizations, and institutions and individuals from many countries.

5. The sources of conflict and war are pervasive and deep. To reach them will require the utmost effort to enhance respect for human rights and fundamental freedoms, to promote sustainable economic and social development for wider prosperity. The United Nations Conference on Environment and Development, the largest summit ever held, had a meeting in Rio de Janeiro. In 1994, Population and Development were addressed. In 1995 the World Conference on Women took place, and a World Summit for Social Development has been proposed. I bear them all in mind.

6. The manifest desire of the membership to work together is a new source of strength in our common endeavor. Success is far from certain,

however. While this address ways to improve the Organization's capacity to pursue and preserve peace, it is crucial for all Member States to bear in mind that the search for improved mechanisms and techniques will be of little significance unless this new spirit of commonality is propelled by the will to take the hard decisions demanded by this time of opportunity.

7. It is therefore with a sense hope that the readers take some ideas from this book, and apply them to their everyday life and maybe...racism can be defeated.

I. The Changing Context

8. In the course of the past few years the immense ideological barrier that for decades gave rise to distrust and hostility and the terrible tools of destruction that were their inseparable companions has collapsed. Even as the issues between States north and south grow more acute, and call for attention at the highest levels of government, the improvement in relations between States east and west affords new possibilities, some already realized, to meet successfully threats to common security.

9. Authoritarian regimes have given way to more democratic forces and responsive governments. The form, scope and intensity of these processes differ from Latin America to Africa to Europe to Asia, but they are sufficiently similar to indicate a global phenomenon. Parallel to these political changes, many states are seeking more open

forms of economic policy, creating a world wide sense of dynamism and movement.

10. To the hundreds of millions who gained their independence in the surge of decolonization following the creation of the United Nations, have been added millions more who have recently gained freedom. Once again new states are taking their seats in the General Assembly. Their arrival reconfirms the importance and indispensability of the sovereign State as the fundamental entity of the international community.

11. We have entered a time of global transition marked by uniquely contradictory trends. Regional and continental associations of states are evolving ways to deepen cooperation and ease some of the contentious characteristics of sovereign and nationalistic rivalries. National boundaries are blurred by advanced communications and global commerce, and by the decisions of states to yield some sovereign prerogatives to larger, common political associations. At the same time, however, fierce new assertions of nationalism and sovereignty spring up, and the cohesion of states is threatened by brutal ethnic, religious, social, cultural or linguistic strife. Social peace is challenged on the one hand by new assertions of discrimination and exclusion and, on the other, by acts of terrorism seeking to undermine evolution and change through democratic means.

12. The concept of peace is easy to grasp; that of international security is more complex, for a

pattern of contradictions has arisen here as well. As major nuclear powers have begun to negotiate arms reduction agreements, the proliferation of weapons of mass destruction threatens to increase and conventional arms continue to be amassed in many parts of the world. As racism becomes recognized for the destructive force it is and as apartheid is being dismantled, new racial tensions are rising and finding expression in violence.

Technological advances are altering the nature and the expectation of life all over the globe. The revolution in communications has united the world in awareness, in aspiration and in greater solidarity against injustice. But progress also brings new risks for stability: ecological damage, disruption of family and community life, greater intrusion into the lives and rights of individuals.

13. This new dimension of insecurity must not be allowed to obscure the continuing and devastating problems of unchecked population growth, crushing debt burdens, barriers to trade, drugs and the growing disparity between rich and poor. Poverty, disease, famine, oppression and despair abound, joining to produce 17 million refugees, 20 million displaced persons and massive migrations of peoples within and beyond national borders. These are both sources and consequences of conflict that require the ceaseless attention and the highest priority in the efforts of the United Nations. A porous ozone shield could pose a greater threat to an exposed population than a hostile army. Drought and disease can decimate

no less mercilessly than the weapons of war.

So at this moment of renewed opportunity, the efforts of the Organization to build peace, stability and security must encompass matters beyond military threats in order to break the fetters of strife and warfare that have characterized the past. But armed conflicts today, as they have throughout history, continue to bring fear and horror to humanity, requiring our urgent involvement to try to prevent, contain and bring them to an end.

14. Since the creation of the United Nations in 1945, over 100 major conflicts around the world have left some 20 million dead. The United Nations was rendered powerless to deal with many of these crises because of the vetoes - 279 of them - cast in the Security Council, which were a vivid expression of the divisions of that period.

15. With the end of the Cold War there have been no such vetoes since 31 May 1990, and demands on the United Nations have surged. Its security arm, once disabled by circumstances it was not created or equipped to control, has emerged as a central instrument for the prevention and resolution of conflicts and for the preservation of peace. Our aims must be:

- To seek to identify at the earliest possible stage situations that could produce conflict, and to try through diplomacy to remove the sources of racism before violence results;

- Where conflict erupts, to engage in peacemaking aimed at resolving the issues that have led to conflict;

- Through peace-keeping, to work to preserve peace, however fragile, where fighting has been halted and to assist in implementing agreements achieved by the peacemakers;

- To stand ready to assist in peace-building in its differing contexts: rebuilding the institutions and infrastructures of nations torn by civil war and strife; and building bonds of peaceful mutual benefit among nations formerly at war;

- And in the largest sense, to address the deepest causes of conflict: economic despair, social injustice and political oppression.

It is possible to discern an increasingly common moral perception that spans the world's nations and peoples, and which is finding expression in international laws, many owing their genesis to the work of this Organization.

16. This wider mission for the World Organization will demand the concerted attention and effort of individual States, of regional and non-governmental organizations and of all of the United Nations system, with each of the principal organs functioning in the balance and harmony that the Charter requires. The Security Council has been assigned by all Member States the primary responsibility for the maintenance of international peace and security under the

Charter. In its broadest sense this responsibility must be shared by the General Assembly and by all the functional elements of the world Organization. Each has a special and indispensable role to play in an integrated approach to human security. The Secretary-General's contribution rests on the pattern of trust and cooperation established between him and the deliberative organs of the United Nations.

17. The foundation-stone of this work is and must remain the State. Respect for its fundamental sovereignty and integrity are crucial to any common international progress. The time of absolute and exclusive sovereignty, however, has passed; its theory was never matched by reality. It is the task of leaders of States today to understand this and to find a balance between the needs of good internal governance and the requirements of an ever more interdependent world. Commerce, communications and environmental matters transcend administrative borders; but inside those borders is where individuals carry out the first order of their economic, political and social lives.

    The United Nations has not closed its door. Yet if every ethnic, religious or linguistic group claimed statehood, there would be no limit to fragmentation, and peace, security and economic well-being for all would become ever more difficult to achieve.

18. One requirement for solutions to these problems lies in commitment to human rights with a special

sensitivity to those of minorities, whether ethnic, religious, social or linguistic. The League of Nations provided machinery for the international protection of minorities. The General Assembly soon will have before it a declaration on the rights of minorities. That instrument, together with the increasingly effective machinery of the United Nations dealing with human rights, should enhance the situation of minorities as well as the stability of states.

19. Globalism and nationalism need not be viewed as opposing trends, doomed to spur each other on to extremes of reaction. The healthy globalization of contemporary life requires in the first instance solid identities and fundamental freedoms. The sovereignty, territorial integrity and independence of states within the established international system, and the principle of self-determination for peoples, both of great value and importance, must not be permitted to work against each other in the period ahead. Respect for democratic principles at all levels of social existence is crucial: in communities, within states and within the community of states. Our constant duty should be to maintain the integrity of each while finding a balanced design for all.

II. Definitions

20. The terms preventive diplomacy, peacemaking and peace-keeping are integral and related as used in this report are defined as follows:

- **Preventive diplomacy** is action to prevent disputes from arising between parties, to prevent existing disputes from escalating into conflicts and to limit the spread of the latter when they occur.

- **Peacemaking** is action to bring hostile parties to agreement, essentially through such peaceful means as those foreseen in Chapter VI of the Charter of the United Nations.

- **Peace-keeping** is the deployment of a United Nations presence in the field, hitherto with the consent of all the parties concerned, normally involving United Nations military and/or police personnel and frequently civilians as well. Peace-keeping is a technique that expands the possibilities for both the prevention of conflict and the making of peace.

21. The present report in addition will address the critically related concept of post-conflict peace-building - action to identify and support structures, which will tend to strengthen and solidify peace in order to avoid a relapse into conflict. Preventive diplomacy seeks to resolve disputes before violence breaks out; peacemaking and peace-keeping are required to halt conflicts and preserve peace once it is attained. If successful, they strengthen the opportunity for post-conflict peace-building, which can prevent the recurrence of violence among nations and peoples.

22. These four areas for action, taken together, and carried out with the backing of all Members, offer

a coherent contribution towards securing peace in the spirit of the Charter. The United Nations has extensive experience not only in these fields, but also in the wider realm of work for peace in which these four fields are set. Initiatives on decolonization, on the environment and sustainable development, on population, on the eradication of disease, on disarmament and on the growth of international law - these and many others have contributed immeasurably to the foundations for a peaceful world. The world has often been rent by conflict and plagued by massive human suffering and deprivation. Yet it would have been far more so without the continuing efforts of the United Nations. This wide experience must be taken into account in assessing the potential of the United Nations in maintaining international security not only in its traditional sense, but also in the new dimensions presented by the era ahead.

III. Preventive Diplomacy

23. The most desirable and efficient employment of diplomacy is to ease tensions before they result in conflict - or, if conflict breaks out, to act swiftly to contain it and resolve its underlying causes.

The Secretary-General may perform preventive diplomacy personally or through senior staff or specialized agencies and programmers, by the Security Council or the General Assembly, and by regional organizations in cooperation with the United Nations. Preventive diplomacy requires measures to create confidence; it needs early warning based on information gathering and informal or formal fact-finding; it may also involve preventive deployment and, in some situations, demilitarized zones.

Measures to Build Confidence.

24. Mutual confidence and good faith are essential to reducing the likelihood of racism and conflict between States. Many such measures are available to Governments that have the will to employ them.

Systematic exchange of military missions, formation of regional or sub regional risk reduction centers, arrangements for the free flow of information, including the monitoring of regional arms agreements, are examples. My hope is regional organizations consider what further confidence-building measures might be applied in their areas and to inform the United Nations of the results.

Fact-Finding

25. Preventive steps must be based upon timely and accurate knowledge of the facts. Beyond this, an understanding of developments and global trends, based on sound analysis, is required. And the willingness to take appropriate preventive action is essential. Given the economic and social roots of many potential conflicts, the information needed by the United Nations now must encompass economic and social trends as well as political developments that may lead to racial tensions.

(a) An increased resort to fact-finding is needed, in accordance with the Charter, initiated either by the Secretary-General, to enable him to meet his responsibilities under the Charter, including Article 99, or by the Security Council or the General Assembly. Various forms may be employed selectively as the situation requires. A request by a State for the sending of a United Nations fact-finding mission to its territory should be considered without undue delay.

(b) Contacts with the Governments of Member States can provide the Secretary-General with detailed information on issues of concerns such as racism among and within States.

(c) Formal fact-finding can be mandated by the Security Council or by the General Assembly, either of which may elect to send a mission under its immediate authority or may invite the Secretary-General to take the necessary steps, including the designation of a Special Envoy. In addition to collecting information on which a decision for further action can be taken, such a mission can in some instances help to defuse a dispute by its presence, indicating to the parties that the Organization, and in particular the Security Council, is actively seized of the matter as a present or potential threat to international security.

(d) In exceptional circumstances the Council may meet away from Headquarters as the Charter provides, in order not only to inform itself directly, but also to bring the authority of the Organization to bear on a given situation.

Early Warning

26. In recent years the United Nations system has been developing a valuable network of early warning systems concerning environmental threats, the risk of nuclear accident, natural disasters, mass movements of populations, the threat of famine and the spread of disease and racism throughout the world.

There is a need, however, to strengthen arrangements in such a manner that information from these sources can be synthesized with political indicators to assess whether a threat to peace exists and to analyze what action might be taken by the United Nations to alleviate it.

This is a process that will continue to require the close cooperation of the various specialized agencies and functional offices of the United Nations. The analyses and recommendations for preventive action that emerge will be made available by me, as appropriate, to the Security Council and other United Nations organs. I recommend in addition that the Security Council invite a reinvigorated and restructured Economic and Social Council to provide reports, in accordance with Article 65 of the Charter, on those economic and social developments that may, unless mitigated, threaten international peace and security.

27. Regional arrangements and organizations have an important role in early warning. Regional organizations that have not yet sought observer status at the United Nations to do so and to be linked, through appropriate arrangements, with the security mechanisms of this Organization.

Preventive deployment

28. United Nations operations in areas of crisis have generally been established after conflict has occurred. The time has come to plan for circumstances warranting preventive deployment, which could take place in a variety of instances and ways.

For example, in conditions of national crisis there could be preventive deployment at the request of the Government or all parties concerned, or with their consent; in inter-State disputes such deployment could take place when two countries feel that a United Nations presence on both sides of their border can discourage hostilities; furthermore, preventive deployment could take place when a country feels threatened and requests the deployment of an appropriate United Nations presence along its side of the border alone. In each situation, the mandate and composition of the United Nations presence would need to be carefully devised and be clear to all.

29. In conditions of crisis within a country, when the Government requests or all parties consent, preventive deployment could help in a number of ways to alleviate suffering and to limit or control violence. Humanitarian assistance, impartially provided, could be of critical importance; assistance in maintaining security, whether through military, police or civilian personnel, could save lives and develop conditions of safety in which negotiations can be held; the United Nations could also help in conciliation efforts if this should be the wish of the parties. In certain circumstances, the United Nations may well need to draw upon the specialized skills and resources of various parts of the United Nations system; such operations may also on occasion require the participation of non-governmental organizations.

30. In these situations of internal crisis the United Nations will need to respect the sovereignty of the State; to do otherwise would not be in accordance with the understanding of Member States in accepting the principles of the Charter. The Organization must remain mindful of the carefully negotiated balance of the guiding principles annexed to General Assembly resolution 46/182 of 19 December 1991.

Those guidelines stressed, inter alias, that humanitarian assistance must be provided in accordance with the principles of humanity, neutrality and impartiality; that the sovereignty, territorial integrity and national unity of states must be fully respected in accordance with the Charter of the United Nations; and that, in this context, humanitarian assistance should be provided with the consent of the affected country and, in principle, on the basis of an appeal by that country. The guidelines also stressed the responsibility of States to take care of the victims of emergencies occurring on their territory and the need for access to those requiring humanitarian assistance. In the light of these guidelines, a Government's request for United Nations involvement, or consent to it, would not be an infringement of that state's sovereignty or be contrary to Article 2, paragraph 7, of the Charter, which refers to matters essentially within the domestic jurisdiction of any state.

31. In inter-state disputes, when both parties agree, the Security Council concludes that the likelihood of hostilities between neighboring countries could be removed by the preventive deployment of a United Nations presence on the territory of each state, such action should be taken. The nature of the tasks to be performed would determine the composition of the United Nations presence.

32. In cases where one nation fears a cross-border attack, if the Security Council concludes that a United Nations presence on one side of the border, with the consent only of the requesting country, would serve to deter conflict, I recommend that preventive deployment take place. Here again, the specific nature of the situation would determine the mandate and the personnel required to fulfill it.

Demilitarized Zones

33. In the past, demilitarized zones have been established by agreement of the parties at the conclusion of a conflict. In addition to the deployment of United Nations personnel in such zones as part of peace-keeping operations, consideration should now be given to the usefulness of such zones as a form of preventive deployment, on both sides of a border, with the agreement of the two parties, as a means of separating potential belligerents, or on one side of the line, at the request of one party, for the purpose of removing any pretext for attack. Demilitarized zones would serve as symbols of the international community's concern that conflict be prevented.

IV. Peacemaking

34. Between the tasks of seeking to prevent conflict and keeping the peace lays the responsibility to try to bring hostile parties to agreement by peaceful means. Chapter VI of the Charter sets forth a comprehensive list of such means for the resolution of conflict. These have been amplified in various declarations adopted by the General Assembly, including the Manila Declaration of 1982 on the Peaceful Settlement of International Disputes and the 1988 Declaration on the Prevention and Removal of Disputes and Situations, which may threaten International Peace and Security, and on the Role of the United Nations in this Field. They have also been the subject of various resolutions of the General

Assembly, including resolution 44/21 of 15 November 1989 on enhancing international peace, security and international cooperation in all its aspects in accordance with the Charter of the United Nations. The United Nations has had wide experience in the application of these peaceful means. If conflicts have gone unresolved, it is not because techniques for peaceful settlement were unknown or inadequate. The fault lies first in the lack of political will of parties to seek a solution to their differences through such means as are suggested in Chapter VI of the Charter, and second, in the lack of leverage at the disposal of a third party if this is the procedure chosen. The indifference of the international community to a problem, or the marginalization of it, can also thwart the possibilities of solution. We must look primarily to these areas if we hope to enhance the capacity of the Organization for achieving peaceful settlements.

35. The present determination in the Security Council to resolve international disputes in the manner foreseen in the Charter has opened the way for a more active Council role. With greater unity has come leverage and persuasive power to lead hostile parties towards negotiations. The Council must to take full advantage of the provisions of the Charter under which it may recommend appropriate procedures or methods for dispute settlement and, if all the parties to a dispute so request, make recommendations to the parties for a specific settlement of the dispute.

36. The General Assembly, like the Security Council and the Secretary-General, also has an important role assigned to it under the Charter for the maintenance of international peace and security. As a universal forum, its capacity to consider and recommend appropriate action must be recognized. To that end it is essential to promote its utilization by all Member States so as to bring greater influence to bear in pre-empting or containing situations, which are likely to threaten international peace and security.

37. Mediation and negotiation can be undertaken by an individual designated by the Security Council, by the General Assembly or by the Secretary-General. There is a long history of the utilization by the United Nations of distinguished statesmen to facilitate the processes of peace. They can bring a personal prestige that, in addition to their experience, can encourage the parties to enter serious negotiations.

While the mediator's effectiveness is enhanced by strong and evident support from the Council, the General Assembly and the relevant Member States acting in their national capacity, the good offices of the Secretary-General may at times be employed most effectively when conducted independently of the deliberative bodies. Close and continuous consultation between the Secretary-General and the Security Council is, however, essential to ensure full awareness of how the Council's influence can best be applied and to develop a common strategy for the peaceful settlement of specific disputes.

The World Court

38. The docket of the International Court of Justice has grown fuller but it remains an under-used resource for the peaceful adjudication of disputes. Greater reliance on the Court would be an important contribution to United Nations peace-making. In this connection, I call attention to the power of the Security Council under Articles 36 and 37 of the Charter to recommend to Member States the submission of a dispute to the International Court of Justice, arbitration or other dispute-settlement mechanisms.

39. The recommended steps to reinforce the role of the International Court of Justice:

    (a) All Member States have accepted the general jurisdiction of the International Court under Article 36 of its Statute, without any reservation, before the end of the United Nations Decade of International Law in the year 2000. In instances where domestic structures prevent this, States have agreed bilaterally or multilaterally to a comprehensive list of matters they have submitted to the Court.

    (b) When submission of a dispute to the full Court is not practical, the Chambers jurisdiction should be used;

    (c) States should support the Trust Fund established to assist countries unable to afford the cost involved in bringing a dispute to the Court, and such countries should take full advantage of the Fund in order to resolve their disputes.

Amelioration Through Assistance

40. Peacemaking is at times facilitated by international action to ameliorate circumstances that have contributed to the dispute or conflict. If, for instance, assistance to displaced persons within a society is essential to a solution, then the United Nations should be able to draw upon the resources of all agencies and programs concerned.

At present, there is no adequate mechanism in the United Nations through which the Security Council, the General Assembly or the Secretary-General can mobilize the resources needed for such positive leverage and engage the collective efforts of the United Nations system for the peaceful resolution of a conflict. I have raised this concept in the Administrative Committee on Coordination, which brings together the executive heads of United Nations agencies and programs; we are exploring methods by which the inter-agency system can improve its contribution to the peaceful resolution of disputes.

Sanctions and Special Economic Problems

41. In circumstances when peacemaking requires the imposition of sanctions under Article 41 of the Charter, it is important that States confronted with special economic problems not only have the right

to consult the Security Council regarding such problems, as Article 50 provides, but also have a realistic possibility of having their difficulties addressed.

It is recommended that the Security Council devise a set of measures involving the financial institutions and other components of the United Nations system that can be put in place to insulate States from such difficulties. Such measures would be a matter of equity and a means of encouraging States to cooperate with decisions of the Council.

Use of Military Force

42. It is the essence of the concept of collective security as contained in the Charter that if peaceful means fail, the measures provided in Chapter VII should be used, on the decision of the Security Council, to maintain or restore international peace and security in the face of a "threat to the peace, breach of the peace, or act of aggression". The Security Council has not so far made use of the most coercive of these measures - the action by military force foreseen in Article 42. In the situation between Iraq and Kuwait, the Council chose to authorize Member States to take measures on its behalf.

The Charter, however, provides a detailed approach, which now merits the attention of all Member States.

43. Under Article 42 of the Charter, the Security Council has the authority to take military action to maintain or restore international peace and security. While such action should only be taken when all peaceful means have failed, the option of taking it is essential to the credibility of the United Nations as a guarantor of international security.

This will require bringing into being, through negotiations, the special agreements foreseen in Article 43 of the Charter, whereby Member States undertake to make armed forces, assistance and facilities available to the Security Council for the purposes stated in Article 42, not only on an ad hoc basis but on a permanent basis. Under the political circumstances that now exist for the first time since the Charter was adopted, the long-standing obstacles to the conclusion of such special agreements should no longer prevail. The ready availability of armed forces on call could serve, in itself, as a means of deterring breaches of the peace since a potential aggressor would know that the Council had at its disposal a means of response. Forces under Article 43 may perhaps never be sufficiently large or well enough equipped to deal with a threat from a major army equipped with sophisticated weapons. They would be useful, however, in meeting any threat posed by a military force of a lesser order. It is recommended that the Security Council initiate negotiations in accordance with Article 43, supported by the Military Staff Committee, which may be augmented if necessary by others in accordance with Article 47, paragraph 2, of the Charter.

It is also recommended that the role of the Military Staff Committee should be seen in the context of Chapter VII, and not that of the planning or conduct of peace-keeping operations.

Peace-Enforcement Units

44. The mission of forces under Article 43 would be to respond to outright aggression, imminent or actual. Such forces are not likely to be available for some time to come. Cease-fires have often been agreed to but not complied with, and the United Nations has sometimes been called upon to send forces to restore and maintain the cease-fire. This task can on occasion exceed the mission of peace-keeping forces and the expectations of peace-keeping force contributors. It should be recommended that the Council consider the utilization of peace-enforcement units in clearly defined circumstances and with their terms of reference specified in advance. Such units from Member States would be available on call and would consist of troops that have volunteered for such service.

They would have to be more heavily armed than peace-keeping forces and would need to undergo extensive preparatory training within their national forces. Deployment and operation of such forces would be under the authorization of the Security Council and would, as in the case of peace-keeping forces, be under the command of the Secretary-General. I consider such peace-enforcement units to be warranted as a provisional measure under Article 40 of the Charter. Such peace-enforcement units should not be confused with the forces that may eventually be constituted under Article 43 to deal with acts of aggression or with the military personnel, which Governments may agree to keep on stand-by for possible contribution to peace-keeping operations.

45. Just as diplomacy will continue across the span of all the activities dealt with in the present report, so there may not be a dividing line between peacemaking and peace-keeping. Peacemaking is often a prelude to peace-keeping - just as the deployment of a United Nations presence in the field may expand possibilities for the prevention of conflict, facilitate the work of peacemaking and in many cases serve as a prerequisite for peace-building.

V. Peace-keeping

46. Peace-keeping can rightly be called the invention of the United Nations. It has brought a degree of stability to numerous areas of tension around the world.

Increasing Demands

47. Thirteen peace-keeping operations were established between the years 1945 and 1987; 13 others since then. An estimated 528,000 military, police and civilian personnel had served under the flag of the United Nations until January 1992. Over 800 of them from 43 countries have died in

the service of the Organization. The costs of these operations have aggregated some $8.3 billion till 1992. The unpaid arrears towards them stand at over $800 million, which represents a debt owed by the Organization to the troop-contributing countries.

Peace-keeping operations approved at present (2005) are estimated to cost close to $5 billion in the current 12-month period, while patterns of payment are unacceptably slow. Against this, global defense expenditures at the end of the last decade had approached $1 trillion a year, or $2 million per minute.

48. The contrast between the costs of United Nations peace-keeping and the costs of the alternative, war - between the demands of the Organization and the means provided to meet them - would be farcical were the consequences not so damaging to global stability and to the credibility of the Organization. At a time when nations and peoples increasingly are looking to the United Nations for assistance in keeping the peace - and holding it responsible when this cannot be so - fundamental decisions must be taken to enhance the capacity of the Organization in this innovative and productive exercise of its function. It must be understood that at the present volume and unpredictability of peace-keeping assessments poses real problems for some member states. For this reason, I strongly support proposals in some Member States for their peace-keeping contributions to be financed from defense, rather than foreign affairs, budgets and I recommend such

action to others.

49. The demands on the United Nations for peace-keeping, and peace-building, operations will in the coming years continue to challenge the capacity, the political and financial will, and the creativity of the Secretariat and Member States.

New Departures in Peace-Keeping

50. The nature of peace-keeping operations has evolved rapidly in recent years. The established principles and practices of peace-keeping have responded flexibly to new demands of recent years, and the basic conditions for success remain unchanged: a clear and practicable mandate; the cooperation of the parties in implementing that mandate; the continuing support of the Security Council; the readiness of Member States to contribute the military, police and civilian personnel, including specialists, required; effective United Nations command at Headquarters and in the field; and adequate financial and logistic support. As the international climate has changed and peace-keeping operations are increasingly fielded to help implement settlements that have been negotiated by peacemakers, a new array of demands and problems has emerged regarding logistics, equipment, personnel and finance, all of which could be corrected if Member States so wished and were ready to make the necessary resources available.

Personnel

51. Member States are keen to participate in peace-keeping operations. Military observers and infantry are invariably available in the required numbers, but logistic units present a greater problem, as few armies can afford to spare such units for an extended period.

Member States were requested in 1990 to state what military personnel they were in principle prepared to make available; few replied.

Stand-by arrangements should be confirmed, as appropriate, through exchanges of letters between the Secretariat and Member States concerning the kind and number of skilled personnel they will be prepared to offer the United Nations as the needs of new operations arise.

52. Increasingly, peace-keeping requires that civilian political officers, human rights monitors, electoral officials, refugee and humanitarian aid specialists and police play as central a role as the military. Police personnel have proved increasingly difficult to obtain in the numbers required. It is recommended that arrangements be reviewed and improved for training peace-keeping personnel - civilian, police, or military - using the varied capabilities of Member State Governments, of non-governmental organizations and the facilities of the Secretariat. As efforts go forward to include additional States as contributors, some States with considerable potential should focus on language training for police contingents, which

may serve with the Organization. As for the United Nations itself, special personnel procedures, including incentives, should be instituted to permit the rapid transfer of Secretariat staff members to service with peace-keeping operations. The strength and capability of military staff serving in the Secretariat should be augmented to meet new and heavier requirements.

Logistics

53. Not all Governments can provide their battalions with the equipment they need for service abroad. While some equipment is provided by troop-contributing countries, a great deal has to come from the United Nations, including equipment to fill gaps in under-equipped national units. The United Nations has no standing stock of such equipment. Orders must be placed with manufacturers, which create a number of difficulties. A pre-positioned stock of basic peace-keeping equipment should be established, so that at least some vehicles, communications equipment, generators, etc., would be immediately available at the start of an operation. Alternatively, Governments should commit themselves to keeping certain equipment, specified by the Secretary-General, on stand-by for immediate sale, loan or donation to the United Nations when required.

54. Member States in a position to do so should make air- and sea-lift capacity available to the United Nations free of cost or at lower than commercial

rates, as was the practice until recently.

VI. Post-conflict peace-building

55. Peacemaking and peace-keeping operations, to be truly successful, must come to include comprehensive efforts to identify and support structures which will tend to consolidate peace and advance a sense of confidence and well-being among people. Through agreements ending civil strife, these may include disarming the previously warring parties and the restoration of order, the custody and possible destruction of weapons, repatriating refugees, advisory and training support for security personnel, monitoring elections, advancing efforts to protect human rights, reforming or strengthening governmental institutions and promoting formal and informal processes of political participation.

56. In the aftermath of international war, post-conflict peace-building may take the form of concrete cooperative projects which link two or more countries in a mutually beneficial undertaking that can not only contribute to economic and social development but also enhance the confidence that is so fundamental to peace. For example, projects that bring States together to develop agriculture improve transportation or utilize resources such as water or electricity that they need to share, or joint programs through which barriers between nations are brought down by means of freer travel, cultural exchanges and mutually beneficial youth and educational projects.

Reducing hostile perceptions through educational exchanges and curriculum reform may be essential to forestall a re-emergence of cultural and national tensions, which could spark, renewed hostilities.

57. In surveying the range of efforts for peace, the concept of peace-building as the construction of a new environment should be viewed as the counterpart of preventive diplomacy, which seeks to avoid the breakdown of peaceful conditions. When conflict breaks out, mutually reinforcing efforts at peacemaking and peace-keeping come into play.

Once these have achieved their objectives, only sustained, cooperative work to deal with under-lying economic, social, cultural and humanitarian problems can place an achieved peace on a durable foundation. Preventive diplomacy is to avoid a crisis; post-conflict peace-building is to prevent a recurrence.

58. Increasingly it is evident that peace-building after civil or international strife must address the serious problem of land mines, many tens of millions of which remain scattered in present or former combat zones. De-mining should be emphasized in the terms of reference of peace-keeping operations and is crucially important in the restoration of activity when peace-building is under way: agriculture cannot be revived without de-mining and the restoration of transport may require the laying of hard surface roads to prevent

re-mining. In such instances, the link becomes evident between peace-keeping and peace-building. Just as demilitarized zones may serve the cause of preventive diplomacy and preventive deployment to avoid conflict, so may demilitarization assist in keeping the peace or in post-conflict peace-building, as a measure for heightening the sense of security and encouraging the parties to turn their energies to the work of peaceful restoration of their societies.

59. There is a new requirement for technical assistance, which the United Nations has an obligation to develop and provide when requested: support for the transformation of deficient national structures and capabilities, and for the strengthening of new democratic institutions. The authority of the United Nations system to act in this field would rest on the consensus that social peace is as important as strategic or political peace.

There is an obvious connection between democratic practices - such as the rule of law and transparency in decision-making - and the achievement of true peace and security in any new and stable political order. These elements of good governance need to be promoted at all levels of international and national political communities.

VII. Cooperation with Regional Arrangements and Organizations

60. The Covenant of the League of Nations, in its

Article 21, noted the validity of regional understandings for securing the maintenance of peace. The Charter devotes Chapter VIII to regional arrangements or agencies for dealing with such matters relating to the maintenance of international peace and security as are appropriate for regional action and consistent with the Purposes and Principles of the United Nations. The Cold War impaired the proper use of Chapter VIII and indeed, in that era, regional arrangements worked on occasion against resolving disputes in the manner foreseen in the Charter.

61. The Charter deliberately provides no precise definition of regional arrangements and agencies, thus allowing useful flexibility for undertakings by a group of States to deal with a matter appropriate for regional action, which also could contribute, to the maintenance of international peace and security.

    Such associations or entities could include treaty-based organizations, whether created before or after the founding of the United Nations, regional organizations for mutual security and defense, organizations for general regional development or for cooperation on a particular economic topic or function, and groups created to deal with a specific political, economic or social issue of current concern.

62. In this regard, the United Nations has recently encouraged a rich variety of complementary efforts. Just as no two regions or situations are

the same, so the design of cooperative work and its division of labor must adapt to the realities of each case with flexibility and creativity. In Africa, three different regional groups _ the Organization of African Unity, the League of Arab States and the Organization of the Islamic Conference - joined efforts with the United Nations regarding Somalia. In the Asian context, the Association of South-East Asian Nations and individual States from several regions were brought together with the parties to the Cambodian conflict at an international conference in Paris, to work with the United Nations. For El Salvador, a unique arrangement - The Friends of the Secretary-General - contributed to agreements reached through the mediation of the Secretary-General. The end of the war in Nicaragua involved a highly complex effort which was initiated by leaders of the region and conducted by individual States, groups of States and the Organization of American States. Efforts undertaken by the European Community and its member States, with the support of States participating in the Conference on Security and Cooperation in Europe, have been of central importance in dealing with the crisis in the Balkans and neighboring areas.

63. In the past, regional arrangements often were created because of the absence of a universal system for collective security; thus their activities could on occasion work at cross-purposes with the sense of solidarity required for the effective-ness of the world Organization. But in this new era of opportunity, regional arrangements or

agencies can render great service if their activities are undertaken in a manner consistent with the Purposes and Principles of the Charter, and if Chapter VIII governs their relationship with the United Nations, and particularly the Security Council.

64. It is not the purpose of the present report to set forth any formal pattern of relationship between regional organizations and the United Nations, or to call for any specific division of labor. What is clear, however, is that regional arrangements or agencies in many cases possess a potential that should be utilized in serving the functions covered in this report: preventive diplomacy, peace-keeping, peacemaking and post-conflict peace-building.

Under the Charter, the Security Council has and will continue to have primary responsibility for maintaining international peace and security, but regional action as a matter of decentralization, delegation and cooperation with United Nations efforts could not only lighten the burden of the Council but also contribute to a deeper sense of participation, consensus and democratization in international affairs.

65. Regional arrangements and agencies have not in recent decades been considered in this light, even when originally designed in part for a role in maintaining or restoring peace within their regions of the world. Today a new sense exists that they have contributions to make. Consultations between the United Nations and regional

arrangements or agencies could do much to build international consensus on the nature of a problem and the measures required to address it. Regional organizations participating in complementary efforts with the United Nations in joint undertakings would encourage States outside the region to act supportively. And should the Security Council choose specifically to authorize a regional arrangement or organization to take the lead in addressing a crisis within its region, it could serve to lend the weight of the United Nations to the validity of the regional effort. Carried forward in the spirit of the Charter, and as envisioned in Chapter VIII, the approach outlined here could strengthen a general sense that democratization is being encouraged at all levels in the task of maintaining international peace and security, it being essential to continue to recognize that the primary responsibility will continue to reside in the Security Council.

VIII. Safety of Personnel

66. When United Nations personnel are deployed in conditions of strife, whether for preventive diplomacy, peacemaking, peace-keeping, peace-building or humanitarian purposes, and the need arises to ensure their safety. There has been an unconscionable increase in the number of fatalities.

Following the conclusion of a cease-fire and in order to prevent further outbreaks of violence, United Nations guards were called upon to assist in volatile conditions in Iraq. Their presence afforded a measure of security to United Nations personnel and supplies and, in addition, introduced an element of reassurance and stability that helped to prevent renewed conflict.

Depending upon the nature of the situation, different configurations and compositions of security deployments will need to be considered. As the variety and scale of threat widens, innovative measures will be required to deal with the dangers facing United Nations personnel.

67. Experience has demonstrated that the presence of a United Nations operation has not always been sufficient to deter hostile action. Duty in areas of danger can never be risk-free; United Nations personnel must expect to go in harm's way at times. The entire international community should respect the courage, commitment and idealism shown by United Nations personnel. These men and women deserve to be properly recognized and rewarded for the perilous tasks they undertake. Their interests and those of their families must be given due regard and protected.

68. Given the pressing need to afford adequate protection to United Nations personnel engaged in life-endangering circumstances, It is recommended that the Security Council, unless it elects immediately to withdraw the United Nations presence in order to preserve the credibility of the Organization, gravely consider what action should be taken towards those who put United Nations personnel in danger. Before deployment takes place, the Council should keep open the option of

considering in advance collective measures, possibly including those under Chapter VII when a threat to international peace and security is also involved, to come into effect should the purpose of the United Nations operation systematically be frustrated and hostilities occur.

IX. Financing

69. A chasm has developed between the tasks entrusted to this Organization and the financial means provided to it. The truth of the matter is that our vision cannot really extend to the prospect opening before us as long as our financing remains myopic. There are two main areas of concern: the ability of the Organization to function over the longer term; and immediate requirements to respond to a crisis.

70. To remedy the financial situation of the United Nations in all its aspects, repeatedly drew the attention of Member States to the increasingly impossible situation that has arisen and, during the forty-sixth session of the General Assembly, made a number of proposals. Those proposals, which remain before the Assembly, are the following:

- *Proposal one:* This suggested the adoption of a set of measures to deal with the cash flow problems caused by the exceptionally high level of unpaid contributions as well as with the problem of inadequate working capital reserves:

(a) Charging interest on the amounts of assessed contributions that are not paid on time;

(b) Suspending certain financial regulations of the United Nations to permit the retention of budgetary surpluses;

(c) Increasing the Working Capital Fund to a level of $250 million and endorsing the principle that the level of the Fund should be approximately 25 per cent of the annual assessment under the regular budget;

(d) Establishment of a temporary Peace-keeping Reserve Fund, at a level of $50 million, to meet initial expenses of peace-keeping operations pending receipt of assessed contributions;

(e) Authorization to the Secretary-General to borrow commercially, should other sources of cash be inadequate.

- *Proposal two:* This suggested the creation of a Humanitarian Revolving Fund in the order of $50 million, to be used in emergency humanitarian situations. The proposal has since been implemented.

- *Proposal three:* This suggested the establishment of a United Nations Peace Endowment Fund, with an initial target of $1 billion. The Fund would be created by a combination of assessed and voluntary contributions, with the latter being sought from Governments, the private sector as well as individuals. Once the Fund reached its target level, the proceeds from the investment of its principal would be used to finance the initial costs of authorized peace-keeping operations, other conflict resolution measures and related activities.

71. In addition to these proposals, others have been added in recent months in the course of public discussion. These ideas include: a levy on arms sales that could be related to maintaining an Arms Register by the United Nations; a levy on international air travel, which is dependent on the maintenance of peace; authorization for the United Nations to borrow from the World Bank and the International Monetary Fund for peace and development are interdependent; general tax exemption for contributions made to the United Nations by foundations, businesses and individuals; and changes in the formula for calculating the scale of assessments for peace-keeping operations.

72. As such ideas are debated, a stark fact remains: the financial foundations of the Organization daily grow weaker, debilitating its political will and practical capacity to undertake new and essential activities. This state of affairs must not continue. Whatever decisions are taken on financing the Organization, there is one inescapable necessity: Member States must pay their assessed contributions in full and on time. Failure to do so

puts them in breach of their obligations under the Charter.

73. In these circumstances and on the assumption that Member States will be ready to finance operations for peace in a manner commensurate with their present, and welcome, readiness to establish them are the following:

   (a) Immediate establishment of a revolving peace-keeping reserve fund of $80 million;

   (b) Agreement that one third of the estimated cost of each new peace-keeping operation be appropriated by the General Assembly as soon as the Security Council decides to establish the operation; this would give the Secretary-General the necessary commitment authority and assure an adequate cash flow; the balance of the costs would be appropriated after the General Assembly approved the operation's budget;

   (c) Acknowledgement by Member States that, under exceptional circumstances, political and operational considerations may make it necessary for the Secretary-General to employ his authority to place contracts without competitive bidding.

74. Member States wish the Organization to be managed with the utmost efficiency and care. Steps have taken to streamline the Secretariat in order to avoid duplication and overlap while increasing its productivity. Additional changes and

improvements will take place. As regards the United Nations system more widely, I continue to review the situation in consultation with my colleagues in the Administrative Committee on Coordination. The question of assuring financial security to the Organization over the long term is of such importance and complexity that public awareness and support must be heightened. It is important to have a select group of qualified persons of high international repute to examine this entire subject.

X. An Agenda for Peace

75. The nations and peoples of the United Nations are fortunate in a way that those of the League of Nations were not. They have been given a second chance to create the world of our Charter that they were denied. With the Cold War ended we have drawn back from the brink of a confrontation that threatened the world and, too often, paralyzed the Organization.

76. Even as the rest of the world celebrates the restored possibilities, there is a need to ensure that the lessons of the past four decades are learned and that the errors, or variations of them, are not repeated. For there may not be a third opportunity for our planet, which, now for different reasons, remains, endangered.

77. The tasks ahead must engage the energy and attention of all components of the United Nations system - the General Assembly and other principal organs, the agencies and programs.

Each has, in a balanced scheme of things, a role and a responsibility.

78. Never again must the Security Council lose the collegiality that is essential to its proper functioning, an attribute that it has gained after such trial. A genuine sense of consensus deriving from shared interests must govern its work, not the threat of the veto or the power of any group of nations. And it follows that agreement among the permanent members must have the deeper support of the other members of the Council, and the membership more widely, if the Council's decisions are to be effective and endure.

79. The Summit Meeting of the Security Council of 31 January 1992 provided a unique forum for exchanging views and strengthening cooperation. It's highly recommended that the Heads of State and Government of the members of the Council meet in alternate years, just before the general debate commences in the General Assembly. Such sessions would permit exchanges on the challenges and dangers of the moment and stimulate ideas on how the United Nations may best serve to steer change into peaceful courses.

80. Power brings special responsibilities, and temptations. The powerful must resist the dual but opposite calls of unilateralism and isolationism if the United Nations is to succeed. For just as unilateralism at the global or regional level can shake the confidence of others, so can isolationism, whether it results from political choice or constitutional circumstance, enfeeble

the global undertaking. Peace at home and the urgency of rebuilding and strengthening our individual societies necessitate peace abroad and cooperation among nations. The endeavors of the United Nations will require the fullest engagement of all of its Members, large and small, if the present renewed opportunity is to be seized.

81. Democracy within nations requires respect for human rights and fundamental freedoms, as set forth in the Charter. It requires as well a deeper understanding and respect for the rights of minorities and respect for the needs of the more vulnerable groups of society, especially women and children. This is not only a political matter. The social stability needed for productive growth is nurtured by conditions in which people can readily express their will.

For this, strong domestic institutions of participation are essential. Promoting such institutions means promoting the empowerment of the unorganized, the poor, and the marginalized. To this end, the focus of the United Nations should be on the "field", the locations where economic, social and political decisions take effect. The senior United Nations official in each country should be prepared to serve, when needed, and with the consent of the host authorities.

82. Democracy within the family of nations means the application of its principles within the World Organization itself. This requires the fullest consultation, participation and engagement of all States, large and small, in the work of the

Organization. All organs of the United Nations must be accorded, and play, their full and proper role so that the trust of all nations and peoples will be retained and deserved. The principles of the Charter must be applied consistently, not selectively, for if the perception should be of the latter, trust will wane and with it the moral authority which is the greatest and most unique quality of that instrument. Democracy at all levels is essential to attain peace for a new era of prosperity and justice.

83. Trust also requires a sense of confidence that the World Organization will react swiftly, surely and impartially and that it will not be debilitated by political opportunism or by administrative or financial inadequacy. This presupposes a strong, efficient and independent international civil service whose integrity is beyond question and an assured financial basis that lifts the Organization, once and for all, out of its present mendicancy.

84. Just as it is vital that each of the organs of the United Nations employ its capabilities in the balanced and harmonious fashion envisioned in the Charter, peace in the largest sense cannot be accomplished by the United Nations system or by Governments alone. Non-governmental organizations, academic institutions, parliamentarians, business and professional communities, the media and the public at large must all be involved.

This will strengthen the World Organization's ability to reflect the concerns and interests of its widest constituency, and those who become more involved can carry the word of United Nations initiatives and build a deeper understanding of its work.

85. Reform is a continuing process, and improvement can have no limit. Yet there is an expectation, in which we all wish to see fulfilled, that the present phase in the renewal of this Organization. The pace set must therefore be increased if the United Nations is to keep ahead of the acceleration of history that characterizes this age.

86. In sum, The United Nations was created with a great and courageous vision. Now is the time, for its nations and peoples, and the men and women who serve it, to seize the moment for the sake of the future.

XV. *Conclusion*

Is it possible to get to the truth? I guess it depends on who you ask. Until other ethnic groups acknowledges that African Americans are still along way from equality (Welfare does not count) in America, then the debate continues and we are back to where we started…inequality for the African American. As for the international level, world leader's view on racism is too broad and lacks specifics. Although, the U.N. has extended the "olive branch" of collaboration in bringing an end to racism and its atrocities, the policies and procedures continue to lack clarity; thereby leaving the African American to fend for ourselves. So be it!

A War On All Fronts studies the disease of racism, not its cure. Once the disease is acknowledged, only then can the cure be found.

XVI. *Bibliography*

1. Aquirre, A. & J. Turner. (1998). American Ethnicity: The Dynamics and Consequences of Discrimination. Boston: McGraw-Hill.

2. Blalock, H. (1967). *Toward a theory of Minority Group Relations.* NY: Wiley.

3. Daniels, R. & H. Kitano. (1970). *American Racism: Exploration of the Nature of Prejudice.* Englewood Cliffs, NJ: Prentice-Hall

4. Frazier, E. (1957). *Black Bourgeoisie.* NY: Free Press

5. Hall, R. (1977). *Black Separatism and Social Reality: Rhetoric and Reason.* Elmsford, NY: Pergamon Press.

6. Kitano, H. (1997). *Race Relations.* Englewood Cliffs, NJ: Prentice-Hall.

7. Kivel, P. (1996). *Uprooting Racism: How White People Can Work for Racial Justice.* Gabriola Island, BC: New Society Publishers.

8. Moynihan, D. (1965). *The Negro Family: The Case for National Action.* Washington DC: U.S. GPO.

9. Myrdal, G. (1944). *An American Dilemma.* NY: Harper & Row.

10. Oliver, M. & T. Shapiro. (1995). *Black Wealth/White Wealth*. NY: Routledge.

11. Shusta, R., D. Levine, R. Harris & H. Wong. (1995). *Multicultural Law Enforcement*. Englewood Cliffs, NJ: Prentice-Hall.

12. Wilson, W. J. (1978). *Power, Racism, and Privilege*. NY: Macmillan.

About The Author

Anthony P. Johnson is a Ph.D. candidate in the Department of Conflict Analysis and Resolution at Nova Southeastern University in Ft. Lauderdale, Florida. He received his B.A. in Political Science from Cheyney State University and his M.A. in Central Eastern European Studies from LaSalle University. He has taught a variety of courses as a Substitute Teacher for the Philadelphia School District, is a GED Instructor and was recommended for the Nobel Peace Prize and twice for the Fulbright Scholarship.

www.ingramcontent.com/pod-product-compliance
Lightning Source LLC
Chambersburg PA
CBHW020542290526
45786CB00002B/1002